Governing Tomorrow's Campus

Governing Tomorrow's Campus

Perspectives and Agendas

Jack H. Schuster
Lynn H. Miller
and
Associates

AMERICAN COUNCIL
ON EDUCATION  MACMILLAN
PUBLISHING COMPANY

New York

Collier Macmillan Publishers
London

Copyright 1989 by American Council on Education and Macmillan Publishing
Company, A Division of Macmillan, Inc.

Macmillan Publishing Company
866 Third Avenue, New York, N.Y. 10022

Collier Macmillan Canada, Inc.

Library of Congress Catalog Card Number: 89–30826

Printed in the United States of America

printing number
1   2   3   4   5   6   7   8   9   10

Library of Congress Cataloging in Publication Data

Schuster, Jack H.
    Governing tomorrow's campus: perspectives and agendas / Jack H.
Schuster, Lynn H. Miller, and associates.
        p.   cm.—(The American Council on Education/Macmillan series
on higher education)
    Includes index.
    ISBN 0-02-897372-0
    1. Universities and colleges—United States—Administration.
2. Teacher participation in administration—United States.
3. Collective bargaining—College teachers—United States.
I. Miller, Lynn H.   II. Title.   III. Series: American Council on
Education/Macmillan series in higher education.
LB2341.S3154   1989
378.73—dc19   89–30826
                                                         CIP

Contents

Preface

Campus governance, it is argued at various points in the following pages, is a topic of ever-crucial importance to academic life. Yet, strangely, the topic has been much neglected in recent years in discussions dealing with the state of academe in the United States, perhaps simply because, as we note below, other issues have been pushed to the fore. This collection of essays seeks to be a partial remedy to that neglect.

The inspiration for this volume grew out of a symposium held at Temple University on February 4 and 5, 1988, entitled "Shared Governance in the Modern University." Eight of the authors represented in the following essays addressed that meeting, whose participants were principally members of Temple's faculty, administration, and board of trustees. Their contributions here are similar to those they made at the symposium, although in every case their papers have been substantially revised for publication. The contributions of the six other authors flesh out the subject more fully, reflecting the expertise of their own diverse experiences in matters of campus governance.

The real inspiration for the Temple symposium came from the provocative and often original quality of what the participants had to say about this subject, which has received scant consideration in writings on American higher education during the 1980s. After a spate of attention in the late 1960s and early 1970s to the impact of student activism on colleges and universities, there followed a period of concern with the then-emerging development of faculty collective bargaining and, more recently, with questions of effective leadership at our institutions of higher learning. If, as we believe, it is once again time to focus on questions of who now shares and will share in campus governance, that is not because there has been much in the way of major innovations in governance *structures* on American campuses in recent years. Now is the time for a new look at these issues because changes in governance *functions* are well underway.

Creeping societal change—change often scarcely visible to the semi-attentive—is establishing patterns and trends that impact substantially on much of the received wisdom regarding campus governance, including even the assumptions made by many when collective bargaining first entered the higher education picture in the late 1960s. One theme of this volume, then, most evident in Part I but running as a thread through many other chapters as well, is the effort to discern those trends as a prerequisite to considering how tomorrow's campus will and should be governed.

A second theme, apparent in Part II, is the development and application of newly relevant theories to questions of campus governance. As issues and agendas change, so should our understanding of what is at stake in the connection between the purposes of higher education and how our campuses are run. Each of the contributors to this section offers a distinctive and insightful perspective on that connection; each reminds us of the uniqueness of the American campus as an organizational system, and of the reasons it is unique.

The special province of the faculty within that organizational system is, of course, much of what makes a college or university organizationally unique, and a consideration of the faculty's role is both the central theme of Part III and a major undercurrent in a number of the other chapters. Perhaps some romanticism has been attached to the view that, from their origin in the Middle Ages, universities were almost exclusively under the control of their faculties; still, the functional authority of the faculty's role in governance has seemed by many (especially faculty members) to be under siege from all directions in recent years. That is an issue explored here, complete with warnings and advice.

A fourth theme entails an examination of the impact of various new, external actors and forces on campus governance. This is the focus of the essays in Parts IV and V, in which contributors with much relevant experience consider answers to the question of how college and university government is being affected by collective bargaining (and vice versa), donors, alumni groups, state boards of education, the federal government, other groups external to the campus, and the force of general social change.

The symposium that inspired this volume was itself an indirect product of some of the characteristic forces that have beset American colleges and universities in recent years. It was part of an effort by Temple's faculty senate and its faculty union to end a divisive period within the university, and was sponsored additionally by the university's president and provost. Temple's recent history had included the retrenchment of tenured faculty members by the administration and board of trustees, censure of the university for that action by Committee A of the American Association of University Professors (AAUP), a strike by faculty members within the collective-bargaining unit of the university, and an effort by the faculty senate to ensure an appropriate faculty hearing in case of future termination of appointments through retrenchment.

Other colleges and universities have been confronted with at least some of these kinds of experiences in recent years, so much so that the trends producing them have typified, to a great extent, the problems of the 1980s in American higher education. As the chapters that follow make clear, these are the kinds of issues that are shaping the way tomorrow's campuses will be governed.

We are pleased to acknowledge those who have assisted and encouraged us in this project, including especially Lloyd Chilton, Executive Editor of the Macmillan Publishing Company, and James J. Murray, Director, Division of Advancement of the American Council of Education. We are grateful to the Teachers Insurance and Annuity Association–College Retirement Equities Fund, and especially to Peggy Heim, TIAA–CREF's Senior Research Officer, for support in preparing the book for publication. The Temple University symposium that inspired this volume was organized by a group of Temple University faculty members under the remarkable leadership of Professor Herbert Bass. We express our appreciation to all of them.

Jack H. Schuster,
Claremont, California
Lynn H. Miller,
Philadelphia, Pennsylvania

The Contributors

ROBERT BERDAHL is Professor of Higher Education at the University of Maryland and a Project Director at the National Center for Postsecondary Governance and Finance. A political scientist, he has taught at San Francisco State University, the State University of New York at Buffalo, and the University of Maryland. Specializing in the study of relations between higher education and governments at national and state levels, Dr. Berdahl's books and articles treat British, Canadian, and American aspects of this subject. He has acted as a consultant on state planning and coordination in seventeen states, has served on task forces of the Education Commission of the States, and has worked as a Senior Fellow at the Carnegie Council on Policy Studies in Higher Education. He has served as North American Editor of the journal *Higher Education,* and as President of the Association for the Study of Higher Education.

ROBERT BIRNBAUM is Associate Director of the National Center for Postsecondary Governance and Research, and Professor of Higher Education, at Teachers College, Columbia University. He has served in a number of administrative positions, including Vice Chancellor of the City University of New York, Vice Chancellor of the New Jersey Department of Higher Education, and Chancellor of the University of Wisconsin–Oshkosh. His recent books include *Creative Academic Bargaining* (Teachers College Press, 1980), *Maintaining Diversity in Higher Education* (Jossey-Bass, 1983), and *How Colleges Work: The Cybernetics of Academic Organization and Leadership* (Jossey-Bass, 1988). Dr. Birnbaum currently directs a five-year longitudinal study of institutional leadership.

ERNEST L. BOYER is President of the Carnegie Foundation for the Advancement of Teaching and Senior Fellow at the Woodrow Wilson School, Princeton University. He is former U.S. Commissioner of Education. Dr. Boyer has served as Academic Dean at Upland College in California, as a teacher at Loyola University in Los Angeles, as head of the Commission to Improve the Education of Teachers, for the Western College Association, and as Director of the Center for Coordinated Education at the University of California at Santa Barbara. In 1965 he joined the State University of New York and became Chancellor in 1970. He has authored two major Carnegie Foundation studies, *High School* and *College.* He has been named to national commissions by three Presidents and was awarded a Fulbright Fellowship in 1984.

CHESTER E. FINN, JR., is Professor of Education and Public Policy at Vanderbilt University and heads the Educational Excellence Network from the university's Washington, D.C., office. He served from 1985 to 1988 as Assistant Secretary for Educational Research and Improvement and Counselor to the Secretary of the U.S. Department of Education. Dr. Finn's books are *What Do Our 17-Year-Olds Know?* (with Diane Ravitch, Harper & Row, 1987); *Challenge to the Humanities* (with Diane Ravitch and P. Holley Roberts, Holmes & Meier, 1985); *Against Mediocrity: The Humanities in America's High Schools* (with Diane Ravitch and Robert T. Fancher, Holmes & Meier, 1984); *Scholars, Dollars, and Bureaucrats* (Brookings, 1978); *Public Policy and Private Higher Education* (with David W. Breneman, Brookings, 1978); and *Education and the Presidency* (D. C. Heath, 1977). He has published more than one hundred articles in such periodicals as *The Public Interest, Phi Delta Kappa, The Wall Street Journal,* and *Commentary.*

GEORGE KELLER is Senior Fellow at the University of Pennsylvania's Graduate School of Education, where he teaches in the Ph.D. program in higher education. Dr. Keller has served as a faculty member and dean at Columbia University, a presidential assistant to the Chancellor of the State University of New York and the University of Maryland, and a higher education consultant as senior vice president of the Barton-Gillet Company. He has authored more than one hundred articles and reviews; his latest book, *Academic Strategy,* was cited in a *New York Times* survey of educators as the book that most influenced them. His several awards include *Atlantic* magazine's education writer of the year, the U.S. Steel Foundation's medal for "distinguished service to higher education," and the 1988 Casey Award from the Society for College and University Planning for distinguished achievement in the field of planning.

BARBARA A. LEE is Associate Professor and Director of the Graduate Program in Industrial Relations and Human Resources at Rutgers University. She has been a staff member of the Carnégie Foundation for the Advancement of Teaching and the Office of Postsecondary Education, U.S. Department of Education. She also served as a member of the NIE Study Group on the Condition of Excellence in American Higher Education. Dr. Lee is the co-author (with George LaNoue) of *Academics in Court: The Consequences of Academic Discrimination Litigation* (University of Michigan Press, 1987), and is collaborating with Professor LaNoue on a handbook on faculty employment relations in higher education, to be published by Jossey-Bass. She is the vice-chair of the editorial board of the *Journal of College and University Law,* and serves on the editorial boards of several higher education and law journals.

WALTER P. METZGER has been Professor of American History at Columbia University for nearly four decades. A specialist in intellectual and social history, he is the author of the classic work *Development of Academic Freedom in the Age of the University.* A sample of Dr. Metzger's numerous writings devoted to the history of the academic profession include *Freedom and Order in the University* (with Paul Goodman and John Searle); *Neutrality or Partisanship: A Dilemma of Academic Institution* (with Fritz Machlup); and "The Academic Profession in the United States," in Burton R. Clark (ed.), *The Academic Profession* (Berkeley: The University of California Press, 1987). He is also editor of a forty-volume study, *The Academic Profession in the Modern World* (Ayer Co. Pubs., 1977). He has long served on the A.A.U.P.'s Committee A (Academic Tenure). Dr. Metzger is a fellow of the Center for Advanced Study in the Behavioral Sciences.

LYNN H. MILLER is Professor of Political Science at Temple University. He has also taught at the University of Kansas and the University of California, Los Angeles, and has been Visiting Lecturer at the University of Pennsylvania. A specialist in international politics, he is the author of *Organizing Mankind* (Holbrook Press, 1972) and *Global Order* (Westview Press, 1985), and co-editor of *Reflections on the Cold War* (Temple University Press, 1974). Dr. Miller is currently preparing a revised edition of *Global Order* and is co-authoring (with Lloyd Jensen) a book on international politics. His play on the Alger Hiss case, *The Eye of a Bird,* has been produced in Philadelphia and New York. He has been Associate Dean of

Temple University's Graduate School, and has served as Vice President and President of Temple's Faculty Senate.

KATHRYN MOHRMAN is Dean of Undergraduate Studies and Affiliated Associate Professor at the School of Public Affairs at the University of Maryland, College Park. She is responsible for general education, honors, and academic support of all undergraduates in Maryland's thirteen colleges and schools. Previously, she has been a Guest Scholar at the Brookings Institution, Associate Dean of the College at Brown University, and a senior staff member at the Association of American Colleges. Her speeches and articles focus on the importance of liberal education, the role of adult learners, and the impact of federal policies on undergraduate education. She has served as a trustee of Grinnell College since 1980.

ROBERT M. NIELSEN is Assistant to the President of the American Federation of Teachers for Higher Education. Formerly Associate Professor of Mathematics at the University of Delaware, he is currently Visiting Professor at the University of Texas Lyndon B. Johnson School of Public Affairs.

PATRICIA R. PLANTE is President of the University of Southern Maine. A professor of English before entering academic administration, Dr. Plante was Provost and Vice President for Academic Affairs at Towson State University in Maryland before assuming her current post. She is the author of *The Art of Decision Making* (ACE/Macmillan, 1987) and of numerous articles that have appeared in such journals as *Academe, Change,* and *The Educational Record.* She is now at work with Robert L. Caret on a work entitled *Academic Administration: Myths and Reality,* to be published by ACE/ Macmillan in 1990.

IRWIN H. POLISHOOK, Professor of History at Lehman College, City University of New York, is president of the Professional Staff Congress, the faculty union of CUNY, a vice president of the 665,000-member American Federation of Teachers/AFL–CIO, and chairman of its National Advisory Commission on Higher Education. Dr. Polishook's publications include *Roger Williams, John Cotton and Religious Freedom* (1967); *Rhode Island and the Union, 1774–1790* (1969); and *Aspects of Early New York Society and Politics* (1974); as well as other works of early American history and in the fields of education and unionization. He served on the New York State Board of Regents Bicentennial Commission (1984–85) and on the Commissioner's Task Force on the Teaching Profession (1987–88).

JACK H. SCHUSTER is Professor of Education and Public Policy at the Claremont Graduate School, where he directs the Ph.D. program in higher education. He has been a Guest Scholar in the Governmental Studies Program at the Brookings Institution and a Visiting Scholar at the Center for the Study of Higher Education at the University of Michigan–Ann Arbor. Co-author (with Howard Bowen) of *American Professors* (Oxford University Press, 1986), he is co-editor (with Daniel W. Wheeler) of *Enhancing Faculty Careers* (Jossey-Bass, in press). Dr. Schuster is active in the American Association of University Professors at national and state levels. He chairs the AAUP's Committee T (on College and University Government) and is a member of the association's National Council and Executive Committee. He serves on several editorial boards.

IRVING J. SPITZBERG writes about higher education from time to time. He has edited *The Exchange of Expertise* and *Universities and the New International Order*. He wrote *Racial Politics in Little Rock*. He has written a number of articles about the governance of universities and of other institutions. He has also engaged in governance on occasion as General Secretary of the AAUP and Executive Director of the Council for Liberal Learning. He is currently involved in research about leadership, having just finished directing the Luce Leadership Project, which has created a national network of scholars and leadership developers. He has been a professor and/or dean at SUNY/Buffalo, the Claremont Colleges, and Brown University.

Governing Tomorrow's Campus

I

The Context of Contemporary Campus Governance

If, as seems woefully true, American academics are seldom given more than cursory training in how to teach, their education in the governance of our institutions of higher learning is typically almost nonexistent. While they are graduate students, they may at least receive a knockabout apprenticeship of sorts to teaching mentors; far less often do they observe or have cause to consider their future participation in academic governance as part of the profession for which they are preparing. This absence of serious attention to the rule of the academy no doubt mystifies still further a subject that remains arcane enough, even to those who have attempted to penetrate its mysteries.

Whatever snippets of information these future academics may glean while educating themselves for their careers almost certainly confuse by telling them (a) that professors are nearly sovereign in their own classrooms; (b) that departments are collegial bodies with a great deal of collective authority over curriculur, hiring, and promotion decisions; (c) that, nonetheless, deans and college presidents—and, less frequently, department chairs—retain a formidable authority to overrule collegial decisions; and (d) that even these officers are subordinate to those unseen regents or trustees whose final authority was likely conferred on them because of their business acumen, political connections, inordinate wealth, or some other attribute of the successful life— but never because of their training in the governance of colleges.

Such observations may confound not only the novice academic but also the interested outsider, including even those rare few from beyond the academy who, as trustees and regents, rule over an organization their experience has not equipped them to understand. From bewilderment on both sides may grow apathy, anger, or frustration, some of which, at least, might be avoided if all participants in governance—from the greenest instructor to the grayest trustee—were to undertake a short course in the history of academic governance.

An excellent place to start such a survey would be with the opening chapter of this volume. Walter P. Metzger's evolutionary perspective shows us that, although our American governance forms are sui generis, they possess shared ancestors with those of Europe, and their uniqueness represents a remarkable adaptation to the unique American environment.

Metzger's *tour d'horizon* of our origins in late medieval Europe through our establishment on the North American continent contains many other insights as well, which combine to provide a base for the essays and analyses that follow in the rest of this volume. He explores the likely reasons for the development of the lay board of trustees in American colleges and universities, and for the frequent "privatization" of control over our academic institutions. He suggests that both trends help explain the historic exclusion of the faculty from governance of the institutions in which they serve. Metzger's command of his subject may nearly mask his erudition in these matters—but not his ability to demystify a complex history.

Chapter

1

Academic Governance
An Evolutionary Perspective
Walter P. Metzger

Although I am leery of the boastfulness of disciplines and claim no exclusive boasting rights for my own, I believe that knowledge of the history of academic governance is apt to improve the social science of it, and may work wonders for anyone who confronts the nagging question of how American colleges and universities should be run.

Historical knowledge comes, of course, in a variety of lengths and packages. Like most historians, I fancy that any temporal inquiry, however brief, into any facet of human experience, however small, adds something to general enlightenment. Still, even a dedicated Clio-patriot would not contend that finding the immediate antecedents of faculty grievance committees or the proximate causes of the last decline in federal spending on higher education contributes much to an overall understanding of academic governance. In my view, history is at its heuristic best not when it focuses on discrete operational devices employed by either insiders or outsiders, but when it contemplates gestalts—patterns of academic power relationships that have internal and external manifestations—and when it undertakes to show over suitable sweeps of time how these relationships came to pass. At its most illuminating, a history of academic governance is a developmental analysis of basic interactive forms.

In framing an agenda for this kind of study, one tends to gravitate, wittingly or not, to the language of evolutionary science. Obviously, since academic governance, like civil government, is an artifact of culture and not an outcome of the genes, there is a gulf between history and biology that a borrowed vocabulary cannot bridge. Even so, I believe that borrowing from one realm of discourse to get one's bearings in another—provided it is a deliberate appropriation, with full qualifying and tampering rights reserved—has its not-inconsiderable rewards.

Consider one example of how lines of thinking that do not converge may yet form suggestive parallels. No one would suppose for a moment that forms of academic governance mate with one another, transmit coded replicas of themselves to offspring, or keep other forms from encroaching on their territory by outbreeding them. Forms of academic governance may have complicated tables of organization but, as far as any microscope has discerned, they do not (yet?) have reproductive cells. Nevertheless, one may observe with the help of borrowed lenses that a particular form of governance, once it becomes institutionalized, does tend by virtue of its staying power to pass from generation to generation, that the form present at the delivery of an academic institution is very likely to become entrenched in its host thereafter, and that a form noted for its midwife capabilities is likely to flourish in a country noted for its high rate of institutional births. I doubt that the submerged demography of this subject would be nearly as visible to the historian's unaided eye.

My borrowings from the evolutionary bank of themes and images hint at answers to three prefatory questions about how a broad-scale history of academic governance should be approached:

What should such a history take special pains to explain? The primary and still unfinished business of evolutionary theory is to account for the appearance of new species in a natural universe favorable to the perpetuation of existing ones. Persuaded that a similar bias exists in the academic corner of the social universe, that the survival advantages of precedence and incumbency—of "coming first" and "being there"—work to preserve the status quo, I reason that historians of academic governance, when they encounter novelty (as they do and must), face the same explanatory challenge. "Change" and "continuity" are the staples of all historical inquiry; what is imported by this analogy is the sense that continuity is scrutable and unsurprising, while change is startling and enigmatic, a defiant mystery that waits to be explained.

What forces of change should be highlighted in such a history? Admittedly, evolutionists do not offer much help to historians on this score: genetic variation and mutation will not explain the rise of new forms of academic governance by any stretch of the met-aphorist's imagination. But as an arena in which coherent schemes of explanation battle for acceptance, evolutionary science may teach historians to think systematically about change, if only by impressive example. Thus, the controversy between the gradualists and the catastrophists, a paradigm war that broke out in pre-Darwinian natural science and continues strong in post-Darwinian geology and biology, may suggest an organizing principle, even if it does not function as an answering service that sends out look-alike clues when dialed. In the spirit of that resilient scientific controversy, I distinguish between the piling up of incremental changes that modify and eventually transform a particular system of academic governance, and the occurrence of relatively quick, extreme though not necessarily convulsive, changes in the environment of a going system that kill it off and let a better-adapted one take its place. This distinction writes a job description for historians interested in this line of work: the object of the inquiry, it suggests, is to identify the main accretionary and seismic events in the history of academic governance, to try to explain what set them going, and to decide which events of each type have had the most enduring effects.

When and where should such a history begin? To evolutionary biologists, all organisms are linked to one another in a great chain of being that stretches from one-celled life to man. To historians, the origins of anything cultural must be cultural, not protoplasmic, which is to say, must be manifold and relatively close to present times. Still, the image of the interconnectedness of things through their descent from a common ancestor is as appealing to a historian as to a biologist, and potentially as fruitful, too. I shall assume that the genealogy of American academic governance begins where the genealogy of European academic governance begins—in northern France (for academic institutions below our border, it might be northern Italy) almost eight centuries ago. It is true that, collec-tively, American institutions of higher learning are younger than their European counterparts and tend, in their ceremonies and manners, to live less visibly in the past. But the family trees of their and our systems of academic governance, though they may differ in their more recent branchings, share the very same trunk and are therefore equally old.

A start-to-finish history faithful to this outline would be out of scale in this volume of collected essays. On the other hand, an outline lacking in substance would be like a fruit tart without filling—high in potential, perhaps, but flat in taste. Hoping to land between extremes, I propose to take up two turning point events in the evolution of American academic governance (thus to give the programmed word historical flesh) and to forgo all the others (thus to abide by the sensible rule of comparable girth). The two turning point events were the product of drastic environmental changes that, despite legal continuities, caused the extinction of one type of academic governance and its replacement by another. They exemplify the workings of catastrophic change; gradualistic change, brought on, say, by the bureaucratization of administrations or the professionalization of faculties, will not be examined in these pages, though an understanding of them is also needed to explain why academic governance, with all its inertial tendencies, does not always stay the same.

From the High Middle Ages, when it first emerged, to the Reformation, when it took a major turn, university teaching in the West was a highly privileged occupation.[1] In a turbulent and xenophobic era, when foreign travelers and residents were set upon by country brigands and city mobs, secular rulers issued special decrees to ensure the physical safety of cosmopolitan professors and students (*magistri* and *scholares*) attracted to the universities situated in their domains. In addition, although all of the masters and most of the advanced students were clerks in monastic or minor orders and thus vowed or inured to poverty, they received many material benefits from the good graces of the powerful; witness their excellent showing on the award lists of popes conferring ecclesiastic benefices, and their exemption from taxes and military service by a succession of admiring French and English kings.

But something more than preferment and largesse is implied when it is said that, in this pursuit, membership had its privileges. The masters of the Faculty of Arts in the University of Paris, the most combative of the quartet of faculties in the mother of all the universities of northern Europe, were quick to learn that access to the seats of power did not always shield them from the abusive or intrusive reach of power. A safe conduct pass from the Crown did not protect them from arrest and imprisonment by local keepers of the peace who sided with town against gown when the two engaged in bloody brawls. Repeated appeals to Rome were initially ineffectual in staving off the incursions of the Chancellor of the

Cathedral of Notre Dame, a subordinate of the powerful Paris primate, who asserted the right to grant and revoke academic teaching licenses, to exact oaths of allegiance to his person in order to bend masters to his will, and to try masters for heresy in his own court. It dawned early on this professoriate that the high and mighty would best help those who had legal authority to help themselves. During the thirteenth century, through a series of papal bulls and apostolic decisions, these professors gained the right to be the sole qualifiers and disqualifiers of their members, to write and enforce their own regulatory statutes, to select their own spokesmen and officials, and (with much less certainty) to shift the trial of members charged with criminal, civil, or spiritual offenses from a temporal or episcopal tribunal to an academic court.[2] At the heart of the *privilegia scholastica* lay a form of academic governance that would travel from Paris to all the magisterial universities of the Middle Ages, a complex of autonomies and immunities backed by the fear that the masters of an academic faculty would always be at risk unless they were also masters in their house.

The legal framework for academic governance in the Middle Ages was provided by the device of incorporation. At the University of Paris, each faculty was constituted a body corporate by papal charter and empowered by that legal artifice to use a common seal, sue and be sued as a juridic person, hold and dispose of property in its own name, co-opt and expel its own members, enact internal rules that would have the force of law, and be self-perpetuating unless formally dissolved. As time wore on, charters of incorporation tended less to ratify and extend an existing power arrangement than to found a new institution and fix its governance in one procreative scoop. On the European continent, academic corporate charters would emanate from the Holy Roman Emperor or a crowned head of state as well as from the Vicar of Jesus Christ; in England, a string of papal bulls and royal writs would give corporate status to the masters of Oxford and Cambridge, while the Crown would charter each of their component colleges as charitable corporations set up to execute the wishes of their founder and governed by the fellows and scholars who were the beneficiaries of the gift.[3]

In all its guises, incorporation signified the delegation of significant governmental power to designees who were not a part of government, and significant canonical powers to clerics who were not in the hierarchy of ecclesiastical command. This legal transfer of legislative, administrative, and judicial powers (along with the gift of eternal life) to the *studium* set it apart from the *imperium* and the *sacerdotium*, giving it a precious living and breathing space if not an uncrossable protective zone. Absent this device, the medieval professoriate might well have been absorbed either into the episcopal structure by curial pronouncement or into the emerging state bureaucracies by royal command, and academic governance, rendered spaceless, might never have been able to develop an independent life of its own. The sole means of founding and maintaining universities from the Abelard dawn to the new day that began with Martin Luther, the academic corporation, despite later rivals and alternatives, would leave a deep and enduring mark on the history of academic governance.

This was not obvious during the first two centuries of the Protestant Reformation. In the speckled territories between the Elbe and the Rhine, where often papal charters were annulled, church properties confiscated, and professors required to conform to the confessional preferences of local princes, it seemed for a while that the very idea of a corporate defense against the encapsulation of the academy by the state or church would be repudiated. But when religious passions began to subside, as they did in the eighteenth century with the founding of nonsectarian Halle and Göttingen, and in the nineteenth century when the German universities, led by the University of Berlin, set a premium on freedom of academic research, the corporate ideal was revived. This is not to say that the old order was restored. In Germany, higher education was incorporated into state ministries of education and professors were converted into high-ranking members of the civil service. But the continental system of academic governance, if it by no means went medieval, did forge an effective compromise between the etatist impulse and the tradition of faculty autonomy. In Wilhelmian Germany, where that system attained its best publicized form, the state held the critical power of the purse and had the decisive voice in senior faculty appointments, while the full professors, organized into separate faculties and a common senate, had the power to offer advisory nominations to the minister of education of persons to fill their own ranks and appoint all junior faculty members, to elect their own rector and respective deans, to exercise plenary authority over the award of degrees and the punishment of student misconduct, and to hold office *durante vita*, barring serious offense. In addition, professors were permitted, under the principle of *Lehrfreiheit,* to decide on the content of their lectures and publish the findings of their research without seeking ministerial or ecclesiastical approval or fearing state or church reproof—an exemption from civil service discipline that added an individual zone of immunity to the measured autonomy of the corporate faculties. In that Germany, academic freedom was both a singular and collective noun.[4]

Like their sister universities across the Channel, Oxford and Cambridge were much buffeted by the Reformation. Indeed, in some ways they suffered the harsher blows. Alone among the sovereigns of Europe who opposed the pope, Henry VIII anointed himself pope and invented a state religion, to which the universities, marked by their Roman ecclesiastical ties and cleric membership, were compelled to subscribe. Each of Henry's three offspring brought a different prescriptive canon and church polity to bear on these universities, creating new articles of faith to be sworn to and new batches of dissenters to be expelled. To ensure compliance with the orthodoxy of the moment, the English sovereigns converted the device of visitation, heretofore mainly used by the papacy to settle intractable academic disputes, into a roving royal commission with power to impose religious tests, detect recusants and backsliders, and rewrite academic statutes in line with the wishes of the Crown. Still, despite the tempestuous union of the English state and church that periodically caused academic casualties, the professors at Oxbridge held more firmly to their corporate privileges under the Tudors (and in the next century under the Stuarts) than did their counterparts in Central Europe under the Protestant princes and in Western Europe under the Catholic Valois and Hapsburgs.

In large part, the Oxbridge corporate form was able to weather the Reformation storms because the Oxbridge collegiate structure gained so much tensile strength in that period. Originally set up as hostels for would-be priests whose training was subsidized by bequests, the colleges began to attract a new class of students—the sons of landed or mercantile families who were encouraged by the opening of new state positions to study the *litterae humanores* and were rich enough to pay their way. In the course of the torturous break with Rome, the more pliable college wardens and fellows won greater favor in Tudor courts than the recalcitrant masters of the university; an unusual display of Henrician forbearance allowed the colleges to keep their church lands, the major part of their endowment; the Elizabethan concern for seemly order compelled all students to quit the licentious living halls and take up residence in more respectable college abodes. As a result, although the universities were rechartered as degree-granting institutions in the era of Elizabeth, the colleges became the centers of instruction and administration in the universities, and their charters, reaffirmed by the Crown, vested their fellows with governing powers that went far beyond the husbanding and distributing of bequests. In effect, Oxbridge, rescued from the legal limbo caused by the break with the Mother Church, became a congeries of discrete pedagogical corporations, each empowered to govern itself except as the Crown (or, increasingly, Parliament) would choose to exercise its visitatorial prerogative, a prerogative that the state would not forswear.[5]

Had a European power other than Great Britain succeeded in planting dense settlements in North America during the seventeenth century, the evolution of academic governance in this country might conceivably have run a different course. But fate—which is to say, national rivalries, worldwide wars, map-remaking peace treaties— decreed that the pathway from Paris would be angular, that it would cross over to the British Isles before taking the transatlantic hop. For nonacademic reasons, the English Reformation's approach to academic governance would land here first and would, while struggling to take root, crowd out other possibilities.

The ships that carried the Puritans to the lands of the Massachusetts Bay Company also carried their resolve to found an institution of higher learning modeled after Emmanuel College, Cambridge, a center of learning that would provide as much of that prototype's scholastic, humanistic, and Calvinist knowledge as a transplanted people could recover and a wilderness society could afford. Imbedded in this cargo of ambition was the expectation that the faculty of the New England college, like the faculty of the old England colleges, would be vested with governing powers by a charter of incorporation and that the institution, as befitted a school of the Reformation, would be of one denomination and subject to supervision by the state. Continuity in academic matters was as much a part of these ships' manifests as nonconformity in matters of religion.

Soon after landfall, a college was created—not by a charter of incorporation issued to its teaching fellows, but by a legislative enactment naming an external group of magistrates and ministers as the governing board. This unconventional beginning sprang primarily from the fear that the Anglican king would refuse to charter a college certain to be dominated by dissenters and would not concede that one incorporated body—the Massachusetts Bay Company—had the legal power to incorporate another. At the earliest safe opportunity, which was afforded when the Puritan party took power in England, Harvard did ask the provincial legislature to grant it the right to award academic degrees, a dignity conferred only upon institutions that lived in a state of incorporated grace. In 1650 the General Court issued a charter designating the president, the treasurer, and the five resident tutors of the college as a self-perpetuating corporation with power to manage properties, elect officers, and write laws. At that time only one innovation suggested that the Old World would not be faithfully copied in the New: rather than dispense with the external governing body under which the institution had spent its first fourteen years of life, the General Court kept it alive as a watchdog agency. Now called the Board of Overseers, this lay group had to concur in the actions of the corporation before they could legally take effect.[6]

No college charter was sought in the colonies for the next forty years—not because the colonists weakened in their devotion to that form, but because it took that long for their love of higher learning to offset the drawbacks of its expense. In 1693 the College of William and Mary, impecably Anglican, secured a charter that bore the imprimatur of the king and was thus unquestionably valid. This charter created a corporation of Virginia dignitaries who were to get the college going and then hand over the property and reins of government to a second "body politic and incorporate" composed of a "president" and "masters" who would be the legal personification of the institution. Again, the nonacademic *accoucheurs* were not discharged but given ill-defined supervisory functions as a Board of Visitors, a name that carried a familiar English ring.[7] Seven more colleges were founded prior to the Revolution. All sought and received charters of incorporation. Four charters were drawn up by colonial officials with explicit or implicit royal approval (Princeton, 1746; King's, later Columbia, 1754; Queen's, later Rutgers, 1766; Dartmouth, 1769); the rest were granted by provincial legislatures without that legitimizing stamp but with tacit regal or parliamentary acceptance (Yale, 1701; Philadelphia, later Pennsylvania, 1755; Brown, 1764). All steered clear of the Harvard and the William and Mary duumvirates, which had provoked a great deal of intramural tension, but found other ways to give voice to the interests of the state.

The corporate form of academic governance was a British transplant that would survive the loss of its imperial prop. After independence, all nine colonial college charters, even the royal ones, either remained unaltered and in force or—as in the case of colleges tarred with the Tory brush—were revoked and subsequently restored. Over the next three quarters of a century, the nation would be flooded with wave after wave of new academic enterprises, and the overwhelming majority of these would be chartered as eleemosynary or "private" corporations, authorized by state legislatures that breathed artificial life into the guardianship of donated funds.

It is true that not every academic enterprise in the new nation was of this type. From these academic breeding grounds, which spread from the former colonies on the seaboard to vast newly settled territories west and south, there arose the state university, an institution called into existence by a statutory or constitutional provision, not by a charter of incorporation, and mandated to carry out the will, not of a philanthropic founder, but of the general public expressed through direct legislative acts. In the second generation of American academic institutions—those founded prior to the Jacksonian era—state universities were few in number and sustained in most cases on pauper rations, but in the third and fourth institutional generations, which spanned respectively the rest of the antebellum period and the years between the end of the Civil War and the end of the nineteenth century, state universities became more numerous and more handsomely provided for both by local tax monies and by federal gifts. It bears noting, however, that state universities in America were not part of the apparatus of government or manned by civil servants of the state (this differentiated them from their continental cousins), and were not governed directly by the statehouse in all but certain delimited functions (this differentiated them from political subdivisions like counties and municipalities). Their distinguishing feature was the on-site presence of a governing board and its administrative deputies, a buffer between the legislative parent and supporter and the academy as a whole. Empowered to control property, administer funds, enter into contracts, enact internal rules, and fill every faculty position, it had all the discretionary authority of its chartered counterpart save the right to elect its own members and to be exempt from the application of certain public laws. It was a "public" corporation, public in its primary source of income and in the character of its holdings but corporate in its formal insulation from governmental command. Like private higher education, public higher education would also retain the cradlemarks of the corporate ideal through the years.

Would it be correct, then, to conclude that the key features of academic governance weathered their transposition from one cultural habitat to another without undergoing any basic change? If hardy indifference to milieu has ever been reported in the annals of cultural diffusion, it finds no case in point here. In fact, within the sheath of formal continuity—the retention of the corporation—two transforming departures from the past did take place. The first departure—first to be launched and consummated, first in consequence and abidingness—was the renunciation of the time-entrenched belief that masters (or fellows or professors) were the persons to be incorporated. The institutional changes that ran counter to this belief I shall call "laicization," with the understanding that "laic" here means "nonacademic," not "nonclerical." The second departure, which began after independence and reached its climax in the early nineteenth century, may be called "privatization." Lest current denotations cause confusion, it should be pointed out that the term in this context does not refer to the tendency to sell public assets to private purchasers (in academe, intersector commerce of this sort almost invariably flowed in the reverse direction) nor to a growing share of faculty members, students, or institutions taken by private education (here, too, the long-term trend went the other way), but refers, rather, to the deliverance of the private college from state interference, a movement that purported to evoke a common law tradition but was in fact a variant of the newly arisen ideology of laissez-faire.

Laicization and privatization were not uniquely American trends, but they started earlier and went further in America than anywhere else. Their relatively rapid and extreme development in this locale suggests to the evolutionary historian that they were adaptive responses to sharp changes in the cultural milieu of academic institutions.

To review the history of the establishment of lay control is to be impressed with how quickly the *consortio magistrorum*, the venerable self-government of the masters, became problematic once it disembarked. True, it *was* inserted into the two seventeenth-century colleges, but even there the colonists showed they were of two minds about it. The authors of Harvard's 1650 charter, though they honored tradition by setting up a faculty Corporation, expressed their urge to stray by vesting a nonacademic Board of Overseers with routine veto powers, an action that made it far more of an institutionalized presence than the Oxbridge visitors, with their occasional interventions, had ever been. And in fact, for the first fifty years, the lay board, which asserted its right to appoint the members of the Corporation and fix their salaries, clearly held the upper hand. Still, as long as nonacademic authority was installed in a separate place, academic authority had a rallying ground it could call its own. Harvard's critical deviation did not begin until the Corporation itself turned lay. The recoloring of the membership of the Corporation was facilitated by two ambiguities in the charter: it neglected to indicate whether every Corporation fellow had to be a college tutor, and it did not declare in so many words that every college tutor had to be a Corporation fellow. Before much time went by, these ambiguities were converted into loopholes. From the beginning, when too few tutors were at hand to fill their charter complement, Harvard reached beyond the college's walls for Corporation fellows, usually ministers in nearby parishes. After a while, tutors were appointed with the understanding that they were hired to teach, not govern, a distinction that closed the other door. Finally, by 1780, the Corporation had become faculty-free except for the president; at this point, the Board of Overseers, yielding to a mirror image of itself, began to turn into a vestigial body.

At William and Mary the laity won out, not by infiltrating the corporate body of the faculty but by colliding with it and eventually subduing it. In the 1750s the Visitors, acting on the theory that they were the chartered fount of collegiate authority from whom the masters received revocable powers, began to engage in a series of bitter disputes with the faculty, who resisted what they regarded as a trampling on their charter rights. Only the fact that the English authorities favored the Oxford-trained royalists on the faculty and not the assertive and suspect Virginian gentry on the board of visitors kept these laymen from conquering their academic foes. After the Revolution, the ideal of faculty autonomy no longer had that rod to lean on. In 1790, when a William and Mary professor sued the Visitors for dismissing him and thus depriving him of his right to membership in the Corporation, the argument of the lay board's attorney, John Marshall, that "the will of the Visitors is decisive," prevailed in the state court and thereafter described the College.[8] John Marshall, as we shall see, would have something else to say on the subject of academic governance as the sitting judge in another case.

Long before the seventeenth-century colleges resolved the problems of a dual system in favor of lay control, the eighteenth-century colleges, with a single governing board and a cooler remembrance of things past, sought and received charters of incorporation that named only nonacademics to their boards. In Connecticut, ten clergymen were incorporated as the trustees of what would be called Yale College; they were given undivided power to manage the institution's funds, appoint its presiding officer and its faculty, and even award its degrees (a magisterial function if there ever was one). In New Jersey, Princeton gained the distinction of being the first college to be placed entirely in lay hands by royal authority, the favor being granted in return for the appointment of provincial officials to the governing board. After this, no colonial college charter would provide for faculty membership on the academic governing board.

Of all the characteristics of American academic governance, lay control would prove to be the most resistant to the wearing effects of time. Over the years, the makeup of boards of trustees and regents would change in response to changes in society: magistrates and ministers would give way to lawyers and businessmen; alumni would often gain formal representation; prominent figures in many walks of life would be salted in. But one walk of life—the campus walk on which professors in the home college treaded—would be, with scattered and token exceptions, consistently excluded.

Why did the lay government triumph so decisively and so distinctively in America? A number of answers—all necessarily speculative but some more plausible than others—may suggest themselves if one starts with a prefatory question: why did self-government triumph in the Middle Ages?—and then reasons forward.

It has been widely noted that universities sprang up in Europe just when occupational associations or guilds run by artisan masters for mutual aid and self-protection were taking hold.[9] It may thus be argued that faculty self-regulation succeeded in Europe for as long as it was unexceptional and failed when it became unconventional, giving way, as did all guild organizations in the sphere of work, to the hammer blows of capitalist production. One cannot quarrel with this as a general hypothesis: no type of academic governance is likely to improve its arrival or survival chances if it is perceived as an oddity or an anachronism. But the time-and-place assumptions in this argument do not quite hold up. It was preindustrial America, still innocent of the factory system, still tied to master-apprentice traditions, that abandoned faculty self-government, while industrializing England, with its attenuation of worker skills and its assaults on worker autonomy, held on to collegial self-governance in academe.

It may pay more to be reminded that the *consortio magistrorum* of the Middle Ages was an invention of the Catholic world, indeed of the Catholic Church. The legal privileges and immunities of academic scholars bore a close resemblance to the canonical benefit of clergy: the purpose of both was to protect the empery of the spirit from the empery of the sword, the church from the aggrandizements of the state. As some historians see it, anything stamped with a popish trademark was bound to be greeted with suspicion in so severely Protestant an environment as that of the British colonies. Historians have suggested that John Calvin's Academy in Geneva, the Calvinist universities in Holland, the Presbyterian universities in Scotland, and the Congregational church polity in New England—all examples of tutelary institutions under lay control—gave the colonies Protestant models to pit against a system established in England but derived from Rome.[10] Explanations that emphasize the motivating power of religion make the useful point that, while small changes in academic governance may accumulate without much emotional charge, massive and climactic changes—such as the conquest of the academic corporation by the laity—probably need to be fueled by strong and even passionate opinion. And explanations that point to laic precursors on the fringe of empire or outside the academy but well known to the historical actors have the virtue of reasserting that the new does not proceed from nothing and that familiarity, not strangeness, breeds consent.

But it is doubtful that the laic shift can be wholly attributed to the Protestant connection. This thesis does not account for the fact that lay control was adopted by colleges in varying degrees of religious heat (by Philadelphia, smitten by the Enlightenment, as well as by Princeton, born of the Great Awakening), by colleges with varying gradations of sectarian zeal (by interdenominational Brown as well as strictly Congregational Yale), by colleges tied to hierarchic, as well as nonhierarchic religions (by William and Mary as well as Harvard), and by the worldly and latitudinarian universities that sprang up in the wake of the Revolution. The appeal of lay control was too uniform and enduring to be explained only in terms of the American religious weather, which varied from region to region and over time.

Of all the changes in the cultural environment attributable to migration, one stands out as most directly related to academic governance, most uniformly experienced by diverse ethnic and religious groups, and earliest in appearance. I refer to the decline in the occupational status of college teaching. Unquestionably, the social standing of medieval academics had been very high. In an era when literacy was rare and learning was a special light, the literate and learned masters were presumed to give much back for the privilege of self-government: the tenets of religious faith systematized and cleansed of error, expertise in canon and civil law on which spiritual and temporal administration alike depended, the refound thoughts of the Hellenes, Jews, and Arabs that were added to the Christian store, not to mention advisory, arbitral, and diplomatic services to the royal courts, their own religious orders, and the central church. Compared with their Old World forebears and contemporaries, New World academics did not count intellectually or socially for very much. Undersupplied with educated persons willing to trade a parsonage for a college, enrolling students who were barely of what we would now call high school age for a course of study that was often of pre-academic grade, maintaining residences for students under strict parietal rules, and—always—chronically poor, the colonial colleges were in no position to assemble a mature professoriate. Apart from their presidents, many of whom were recruited from abroad, their teaching and custodial staffs were made up largely of tutors—recent college graduates who paused at the lecterns of alma mater before moving on to pulpits. Although some tutors stayed on for considerable lengths of time and earned the affectionate regard of students, most were transient dons who cut an undistinguished and unhonored figure, and their work lives, if not utterly brutish, were usually laborious and short. For the first hundred and fifty years of American college history, tutors constituted the overwhelming, if gradually declining, majority of all holders of academic posts. Small wonder that the Harvard Overseers treated the Corporation, five-sevenths tutorial, with something less than respect; small wonder that the presidents of Harvard regarded these callow transients as senior sons appointed to help them, the paterfamilias, teach and discipline the younger children;

small wonder the founders of Yale and Princeton would not leave properties and endowments to persons who were so much their social inferiors if only by virtue of their tender age. Moral: a grant of the power to govern not only confers social prestige but acknowledges it, and the Matthew principle—unto everyone that hath shall be given—generally applies here as in other spheres of social life.

In time an esteemed professoriate did grow up in America. By 1800 tutors occupied no more than half of the academic posts in the colleges founded before the Revolution; by the end of the antebellum period, they were wholly eclipsed by professors. From the moment he made his debut as the Hollis Professor of Divinity at Harvard, the American professor stood in sharp contrast to his plainer workfellow—mature where the tutor was green; prominent or at least promising in a discipline where the tutor ran the gamut of subjects on a rudimentary plane; allowed to marry and live off campus, whereas the tutor was unmarried and lived a life immured. In time, within the professorial cadres, there arose research specialists whose contributions to scholarship and science would be highly valued not only in the domestic market but also on the international exchange. Even so, lay control remained ubiquitous and impregnable. Several factors seemed to have prevented late-won prestige from acquiring commensurate formal power. First of all, American institutions of higher learning continued to multiply faster than the pool of academic illuminati could expand, and to precede the development of an adequate feeder school system. These old ways of putting carts before horses would re-create these same demoting pressures that had existed in the past despite the social elevation of the occupation as a whole. Second, the intense competition among small, often shoestring, academic firms that erupted after independence and that would remain (with some upward adjustment of dollar scales) a feature of American academic life, was a deterrent to certain kinds of innovations. For all their standpat reputation, the pre-Civil War colleges were ready to have faculty members experiment with new courses, but were not willing to let them take charge of the college fisc, the risk of a fatal error overcoming any interest in the trial.[11]

After the Civil War, the status arguments for lay control, still operative whenever an institution of higher learning was created by laymen ex nihilo, lost its force in those first-generation colleges that had grown through the years into distinguished universities, and also, after the birthing work was done, in those fourth-gen-eration universities that had been breathed into life by tycoon wealth and had gathered the pick of the nation's scientists and scholars. In these places, efforts by faculty members to gain insti-tutional power, often sparked by dismissal of a professor by a governing board filled with class obsessions or a president who regarded criticism of his policies as a form of lèse majesté, were mounted in the early twentieth century. But lay control was not seriously threatened by this late revival of the academic guild complex. Partly, the failure to re-academize college governance was due to strategic retreats by governing boards and administra-tions (thus, their eventually warm embrace of academic freedom and their grudging acceptance of academic tenure), to the dele-gation of some operational powers and responsibilities to subgroups of faculty members (thus, the recognition of departments of in-struction as resident agents for their disciplines), and to the de-velopment of hybrid roles (the professor-administrant, the teacher as faculty senator) that took the edge off intramural conflicts. But probably most important in protecting lay control from insurgent threats was the impregnable legal position it secured by nesting in the corporation form. The law was permissive about who was eligible for incorporation: at various times and places, students, ethnic groups, recipients of charity had been named. But it became strict in forbidding changes in the composition of an incorporated board once this was inscribed in a legal charter. In the early twentieth century an insurgent movement headed by Columbia psychologist J. McKeen Cattell enrolled a number of professors in the major universities who looked for new ways to govern the academies.[12] But few professors favored the elimination of lay trustees, largely because their fund-raising skills were deemed in-dispensable, but also because their legal position seemed invulner-able, and few academics had a taste for a cause that was bound to fail. Most of the members of this rebellious group settled for whittling the president's office and the presidential ego down to size; after World War I, when the passion for redoing the world was spent, the advocates of a voluntary sharing of authority, some-times called collegial governance, would be alone on the reforming stage until, many decades later and in certain kinds of institutions, support for collective bargaining would arise.

Laicization was the Big Change in this evolutionary story; from this American bough growing on the English limb all kinds of branches would sprout. Only a few of these sproutings can be mentioned here. In the chronicles of old Paris and Oxford, the act of removing a master was commonly referred to as a privation or a banishment, but never as a discharge or dismissal. This terminology is an eloquent reminder that the masters and fellows of the past were not employees of their universities, they were the corporate directors of their universities; not having been hired, they could not be fired, though they could be blackballed by their colleagues (rulerships of peers are not known for their tolerance) and could be cast out from the fellowship (with spiritual pains that may have exceeded those inflicted by mere disemployment). Also, once lay control was established, the concept of academic freedom, at least in the eyes of the organized academic profession, parted company with the continental view of it. In this country, a violation of academic freedom would come to be regarded as something that happens *in* a university to an academic by action of a lay governing board or administration; it would usually not be regarded as something that happens *to* a university by action of a nonacademic outside force, unless that happens also to injure an academic. We passed not only from one type of governance to another, but from one mental universe to another, when we bade farewell to the faculty collegium and said hello to the faculty member enmeshed in employer-employee or (as they would later be called) management-labor relations.

Until rather recently, the growth of privatism was overshadowed by the triumph of laicism in most historical accounts. Today, historians are more aware that it too ranks as a rechannelling event.[13] The idea that the public purpose of a private corporation properly subjected it to public oversight—an idea applied to higher education in the course of the Tudor Reformation—was widely accepted during the colonial period. One sign of its acceptance was the fact that every college charter, with the exception of Yale's, Brown's, and Pennsylvania's, reserved ex officio seats on the governing board for state representatives who, in the unicameral academic setting, would constitute a sizable minority. Some college leaders acceded grudgingly to this kind of permanent visitation as a precaution against estrangements that might jeopardize state financial support; more often, they actively sought the cohabitation of officialdom and ministry, either because it ranged state power on the side of their sectarian founders or because it appeared to offset denominational partisanship and would thus please the Crown.

After the Revolution, when most of the alliances between state and church broke down, politicians found secular reasons for retaining and even reinforcing the public's presence in the inner councils of the private colleges. The Jeffersonian belief that the governing boards of the "elitist" institutions, if allowed to go unsupervised and unchecked, would pose a threat to republican virtue, not to mention Republican party votes, merged with the view of an educational avant-garde that a chartered college left entirely to its own devices would cling to an outmoded and obscurantist curriculum. For a while, this postrevolutionary blend of populism and reformism, spiced by heavy doses of antimonarchic and anti-British patriotism, won out, even in heretofore hostile quarters. Yale's decision in 1792 to accept a charter amendment that placed the governor, the lieutenant governor, and six council members on its governing board, heretofore exclusively composed of Congregational ministers, appeared to mark the fall of one of the last holdouts for the view that a private corporation was "strictly private."[14]

As it turned out, Yale's capitulation (or crafty maneuver by its latitudinarian president to attenuate the voting strength of extreme religionists) would constitute the high-water mark of the effort to translate "private" into "quasi-public." The rapid subsequent success of privatization can be attributed to a trend, a legal case, and a precondition. The trend was the decline of the practical advantages to private colleges of placating the governments of the states. Before the Revolution, with only one exception (New Jersey), no province allowed more than a single college to rise up within its borders. After the Revolution, a change in the political balance of forces and the easing of academic incorporation laws deprived the established colleges of their valued territorial monopolies. In the colonial period, many colleges received land and cash subsidies from the provincial legislatures. After independence, the new states, with more and more mouths clamoring to be fed, increasingly denied all of them the right to sup at their treasuries. As the old quasi-mercantilist system gave way to an open market system, the need to make accommodations to the state was less strongly felt; without the *quid* of public protection and support, the *quo* of public supervision was less apt to gain corporate consent.

That public supervision would need corporate consent in order to be lawful was assured by the outcome of the case of *The Trustees of Dartmouth College* v. *Woodward* (1819), a landmark in the history of academic governance.[15] This case involved the constitutionality of a New Hampshire law that revised the prerevolutionary charter of Dartmouth College, without the consent of its board of trustees, in a way that measurably increased state control. In striking down this law, Chief Justice of the Supreme Court John Marshall held that the states could constitutionally found their own academic institutions and place them entirely under their own control, but that a charter issued to private individuals for objects supported by private funds created private property rights that were protected from state amendment by the contract clause of the Constitution. Later in that century, the contract clause of Section One would yield to the due process clause of the Fourteenth Amendment as the chief constitutional plank protecting private corporations from state intrusion; in the next century, refinements on the concept of "state action" and of businesses "vested with a public interest" would make the constitutional distinction between "private" and "public" less hard-and-fast. But the essentials of the Marshallian decision would have consequences for the history of academic governance that subsequent jurisprudence would not repeal. Accorded the same constitutional guarantees as profit-seeking business firms, nonprofit private colleges and universities would spread like mushrooms and grow like Topsies, mildly checked by accrediting associations but largely beyond the reach of the regulatory and rationalizing functions performed elsewhere by state ministries of education. Moreover, the outcome of the Dartmouth College case would not only encourage the founding of new private colleges (in particular those sponsored and galvanized by evangelic zeal); it would also accelerate the movement toward the establishment of public universities, for it told the states that they had to be the founders of such institutions if they desired to control them, there being no middle ground.[16]

It seems reasonable to suppose that college charters would not have been held to be so inviolable if their recipients had been academics and not laymen. Although Marshall did not say that the identity of the Dartmouth trustees had any bearing on the case, it is difficult to believe that he would have drawn the constitutional line between the *publica* and the *priva* quite so sharply if the salaried teachers at Dartmouth had resisted the efforts of the state to pry open their chamber doors or that he would have been quite so ready to invoke the contract clause to defend a purely scholastic privilege granted by King George III. And it may be argued that the states themselves would probably not have surrendered their seats at the trustees' table if by doing so they would have left the faculty in complete control. It was not, one may assume, a mere coincidence that the laicizing of the corporation preceded rather than followed the privatizing of it.

In a recent article, evolutionary biologist Stephen Jay Gould puts the notion that sequences determine outcomes in a tidy nutshell: "Divert the comet, preserve the dinosaurs, and humans never evolve."[17] His aphorism finds an echo in this story: ditch the corporation and lay control would not have occurred; retain the consortium of the masters and the private college as we know it would not have evolved. But history here introduces a complication: historical happenings do not occur in unilinear sequences; they double back. Lay control helped make the corporation a guiding image for academic governance in the public sector. Privatization combined with lay control gave American colleges and universities the look of extraterritorial enclaves, of islands that were laws unto themselves, that did not significantly change until after World War II, when decisional authority was siphoned in various ways from the local campus to centers of power in the world beyond. If Professor Gould had a mind to mimic history, he would have to say—no doubt against his better judgment—that human beings left their mark on dinosaurs and that dinosaurs made comets more respectable things.

NOTES

1. Pearl Kibre, *Scholarly Privilege in the Middle Ages* (Cambridge: Mediaeval Academy of America, 1962).

2. Hastings Rashdall, *Universities of Europe in the Middle Ages*, Oxford, The Clarendon Press, vol. 1 (new ed., edited by F. M. Powicke and A. B. Emden, 1936); Mary McLaughlin, "Intellectual Freedom and Its Limitations in the University of Paris in the Thirteenth and Four-teenth Centuries" (unpublished Ph.D. dissertation, Columbia University, 1952).

3. Edward Duryea, "Corporate Basis of College and University Govern-ment: A Historical Analysis" (unpublished monograph, 1973); J. A. Burkhardt, "History of the Development of the Law of Corporations," *Notre Dame Lawyer* 4 (1929): 221–43.

4. Fredrich Paulsen, *The German Universities, Their Character and Historical Development* (New York: Macmillan and Co., 1895); Fritz Ringer, *Decline of the German Mandarins* (Cambridge: Harvard University Press, 1969).

5. C. W. Mallett, *A History of the University of Oxford* (New York: Longmans, Green and Co., 1924–27); H. C. Porter, *Reformation and Reaction in Tudor Cambridge* (Cambridge: Cambridge University Press, 1958).

6. Samuel E. Morison, *Three Centuries of Harvard, 1636–1936* (Cambridge: Harvard University Press, 1936).

7. J. E. Kirkpatrick, "The Constitutional Development of the College of William and Mary," *William and Mary Quarterly,* 2nd Series, April 1926, 6:95–108; Florian Bartosic, "With John Marshall from William and Mary to Dartmouth College," Vol. VI, *William and Mary Law Review* 7 (1966):259–66.

8. *Bracken* v. *Visitors of William and Mary College,* 3 Call 574.

9. Sylvia Thrupp, "Gilds," *International Encyclopedia of the Social Sciences* (New York: Macmillan, 1968), pp. 184–187; Henry Pirenne, *A History of Europe* (New York: W. W. Norton & Company, 1939).

10. Edward H. Reisner, "The Origin of Lay University Boards of Control in the United States," *Columbia University Quarterly* 23 (1931): 63–69; Richard Hofstader, *Academic Freedom in the Age of the College* (New York: Columbia University Press, 1955), pp. 120–151.

11. Walter P. Metzger, "The Academic Profession in the United States," in Burton R. Clark, ed., *The Academic Profession: National, Disciplinary and Institutional Settings* (Berkeley: University of California Press, 1987), Chapter 4.

12. J. McKeen Cattell, *University Control* (New York: The Science Press, 1913); M. Sokol, "The Education and Psychological Career of James McKeen Cattell, 1860–1904" (unpublished Ph.D. dissertation, Case Western Reserve, 1972), vol. II.

13. Jurgen Herbst, *From Crisis to Crisis: American College Government, 1636–1819* (Cambridge: Harvard University Press, 1982).

14. Brooks Mather Kelley, *Yale: A History* (New Haven: Yale University Press, 1974), Chapters 6 and 7.

15. 1/ U.S. Report 518–715.

16. Francis N. Stites, *Private Interest and Public Gain: The Dartmouth College Case, 1819* (Amherst: University of Massachusetts Press, 1972).

17. "Mighty Manchester," *New York Review of Books,* Oct. 27, 1988, p. 32.

II

New Perspectives on Campus Governance

American colleges and universities often seem to be baf-
flingly complex organizations, so different from other
organizational systems as to make meaningful comparisons
impossible. The authors of the chapters in this section are
fully aware of the peculiarities of academic governance systems, but each brings an imaginative theoretical perspective
to bear on the subject, and the results are illuminating in a
number of respects.

In Chapter 2, Robert Birnbaum reminds us that, whatever their peculiarities, academic institutions behave in accordance with at least some of the principles of complex,
and especially pluralistic, organizations elsewhere in society.
They contain diverse groups whose interests must be balanced in varying ways. If they are to be governed effectively, that balancing must be accomplished through
considerable sharing of leadership and followership by constituents. Constituent groups must communicate effectively
with each other, for communication is the sine qua non of
the organization's health and viability. Birnbaum's application of cybernetics theory to academic institutions guides
us toward understanding both constraints and possibilities
for campus governance that we may not have considered
before.

Chapter 3 provides Irving Spitzberg's essential reminder
that much of the significant complexity about American

institutions of higher learning lies in their enormous diversity. He presents a typology of academic institutions that allows us, first, to do what Aristotle advised, namely, compare things only as they admit of comparison. In the process, he reminds us of the essential variations in the purposes of academic institutions. But above all, he helps us to imagine the distinctive possibilities each type of institution provides. Those who struggle with the problems and irritations of a particular American college or university should see their situation as like that of the oyster irritated by a grain of sand in its shell. They may respond as the oyster—and the rare academic—has done, in a way that turns their source of friction into a unique and highly prized creation.

In Chapter 4 Kathryn Mohrman sheds new light on the unique relationships between faculty members and those to whom they are ostensibly subordinate both within and outside the academic institution. Revealing many of the reasons why that seeming subordination is very frequently more apparent than real, she applies to academia the theory of principals and agents that has emerged largely from the discipline of economics. She introduces the intriguing concept of "coupled dependency" to the subject as a way of demonstrating how an authority relationship can flow two ways at the same time. As a consequence, she brings persuasive reasoning to bear on her conclusions about the appropriateness of shared governance as a decision-making structure.

Leadership and Followership
The Cybernetics of University Governance
Robert Birnbaum

American colleges and universities are the most paradoxical of organizations. On the one hand, George Keller has said that "they constitute one of the largest industries in the nation but are among the least businesslike and well managed of all organizations."[1] On the other hand, many believe our institutions of higher education exhibit levels of diversity, access, and quality that are without parallel. At a time in which American business and technology suffers an unfavorable trade deficit and is under siege from foreign competition, our colleges and universities enroll large numbers of students from other countries. No wonder we enjoy such a favorable educational balance of trade: the American system of higher education is the envy of the world.

It would appear that we are poorly run but highly effective. The paradox is easily resolved if either one or both of these beliefs about American higher education is wrong. But if they are both right, there are several implications for college and university governance and management. For example, it may be that the success of the system has come about *in spite of* its bad management, and that if management could somehow be improved the system could be made even more effective and efficient than it is today.

Or it may be that, contrary to our traditional expectations, management and performance in colleges and universities are not closely related. If this is true, then attempts to improve management, even if successful, might not yield comparable benefits in institutional accomplishment.

Or, strangest of all, it may be that to at least some extent our colleges and universities are successful *because* they are poorly managed—at least as "management" is often defined in other complex organizations. If this is true, then attempts to "improve" traditional management processes might actually diminish rather than enhance effectiveness in institutions of higher education.

These possibilities have implications for shared governance in the modern university. This chapter will present four related, although admittedly loosely coupled, arguments about the nature of governance and how universities work. To make these arguments manageable, I will simplify and distort the inchoate reality of governance in two important ways. First, I will focus on only two generic roles, the administration and the faculty, even though we know there are many additional and important players in the governance game, both on and off campus. And second, I will talk about these two roles as if they were monoliths, even though our experience is that administrators on any campus may disagree about many things, faculty may disagree about everything, and academic bargaining, where it exists, may itself cause confusion in defining who really is "the faculty."

The Conflict of Roles and Authority in Governance

The first argument has to do with the conflict of roles and authority in governance. It is generally acknowledged that the environment of higher education is more complex and the problems more difficult today than they have been in the past. The tensions of governance and leadership have certainly been exacerbated by new forces related to funding, demographics, and political structures. But the underlying problem has been with us since the time, long ago, when two things happened: being a college professor became a profession, and trustees recognized that complex institutions had to be managed if they were to survive. I cite as witness Thorstein Veblen[2] in 1918, mocking the trustee notion of "efficiency" in higher education in which "these corporations of learning shall set their affairs in order after the pattern of a well-conducted business concern. In this view, the university is conceived as a business house dealing in merchantable knowledge, placed under the governing hand of a captain of erudition, whose office it is to turn the means at hand to account in the largest feasible output."

In contrast, said Veblen, the work of scholars is pursued individually, each in his or her own way. It is not amenable to the orderly and systematic procedures of the administrator, and cannot be reduced to the bottom line of a balance sheet. The administrative role is not to govern scholars, he said, but rather to "stand in the relation of assistants serving the needs and catering to the idiosyncracies of the body of scholars and scientists that make up the university." To the extent this is not done, the university will lose effectiveness because "a free hand is the first and abiding requisite of scholarly and scientific work." Veblen's acerbic comments set forth the enduring governance issue clearly if simplistically: to what extent shall the university be controlled by administrators, who gaze outward and try to ensure that institutions remain stable and responsive to changing economic, political, and social realities; or by faculty, who look inward at their responsibilities to students, colleagues, and the world of ideas?

This conflict was as real when Veblen wrote over seventy years ago as it is today, but it probably has been intensified by the increased scope and complexity of the enterprise. The simple days of amateur management, when faculty temporarily assumed administrative positions and then returned to the classroom, are long since over at most institutions. Because faculty and administrators fill different roles, they encounter and are influenced by different aspects of the environment. As administrative and faculty groups become more specialized, they are likely to become increasingly isolated from each other. Communication between them falters, diminished interaction makes common attitudes less likely, and opportunities to correct stereotypical views of each other dwindle.

Faculty and upper-level administrators are quite similar in many ways but, because of differences in their roles, they may come to see each other as different kinds of people. I will use my own personal experiences as an example. I spent the first seventeen years of my professional career as an administrator in many university settings. My administrative colleagues and I never ceased to marvel at the indifference shown by faculty to institution-wide concerns, their appalling ignorance of the political, social, and economic realities facing their institutions, and their often single-minded pursuit of narrow self-interest. The usual faculty response to proposed change was to arrange the wagons in a circle, so almost all the creative ideas for institutional improvement came from administrative initiatives. But those brave innovations that weren't attacked and willfully distorted one week by the senate executive committee would certainly be so next week by the union negotiating committee. The faculty I spoke with offered simplistic solutions to complex problems, often in terms as wrongheaded and impractical as those of Veblen who, you may remember, suggested that all governance problems could be put to rights by abolishing both presidents and boards of trustees. From where I sat in the executive offices, the issues were clear: the administration had the solutions, and the faculty was the problem.

Ten years ago, when I left administration to become a professor, there occurred, by the strangest of coincidences, a sudden and dramatic change in the governance patterns of higher education. Beginning at that time, and increasingly ever since, it has become clear to me and my faculty colleagues that administrators are responding inappropriately to political and social pressures. They are basing their decisions on fiscal rather than educational grounds, and in the mania for efficiency and accountability they have lost touch with the faculty, with traditional notions of quality, and with the real purposes of the institution. Faculty ideas are ignored, and administrative programs often appear suddenly without proper faculty consultation. Layers of officious technocrats and ambitious deanlets interpose themselves between the faculty and institutional executives; they are no longer even "captains of erudition" but have instead become that most dreaded of all corporate creations, "central administration." From where I sit in my faculty office, I feel powerless. My colleagues and I have much sound counsel to offer, but administrators treat us as part of the problem rather than as part of the solution.

If you resonate to any part of my self-caricature, you are merely reflecting the old aphorism that where we stand depends on where we sit. The differences between faculty and administrators are for the most part created by their roles, not their personalities. On many campuses, if the union president and institutional president were to switch roles (and a university is probably the only organization in which that could, in fact, happen), an objective observer probably would detect little difference. Their disagreements would not change much, although each would now sound much like the other had previously, and the tensions between them would likely continue unabated.

The different environments we confront, and the different colleagues with whom we interact and to whom we respond, lead faculty and administrators to construct different—but equally valid—perceptions of reality. And these different perceptions are themselves reinforced and sustained by the existence in the university of two quite different—but equally valid—systems for organizational control and the assertion of authority. One is the conventional administrative hierarchy supported by the concept of legitimate and legal authority. The other is the structure through which faculty make decisions regarding those aspects of the institution over which they have jurisdiction, which finds its justification in the concept of professional authority.

The basic questions that define a university are who shall teach, what shall be taught, and who shall be taught, but these questions are inexorably connected with matters such as resource allocation, strategy, and accountability. In a business, issues such as these are the responsibility of administrators structured into a hierarchy of power. But in universities, faculty claim the right to primary responsibility for many of these questions on the grounds of professional authority. Administrators are ultimately accountable to their boards; faculty are ultimately accountable to their guilds and their consciences.

Faculty and administrative perspectives are different; indeed, they *must* be different if the institution is to be successful. Without faculty participation in governance, the institution is likely to be sterile; without administrative involvement, the institution can soon become nonresponsive and ineffective. Both perspectives are necessary to guide a mature university. "Governance" is the name we give to the processes we invent to achieve an effective balance of the competing interests of the two structures (hierarchical and collegial) and the two authority systems (administrative and professional). The key word here is "invent"; there are no "official rules," and good governance on any campus is what faculty and administrators on that campus believe it to be.

Leadership and Followership in Governance

The second argument deals with leadership and followership. Normative governance documents such as the Joint Statement on Government of Colleges and Universities[3] suggest that, since the claims to influence of both faculty and administrative groups are valid, the proper relationship between them on such matters is one of shared authority. Accepting the rhetoric of shared authority may be a necessary, but certainly not a sufficient, precondition to good governance, and it does not by itself resolve the tension between the faculty and administration. As General George C. Marshall said, agreement in principle is agreement on nothing, and shared authority is a particularly slippery concept to apply in practice. The fact that some institutions obviously have viable systems of shared authority does not necessarily tell other institutions how they can achieve it. But I believe the essence of shared authority has something to do with the peculiar nature of leaders and followers in the academy.

There are those who argue that leadership in higher education is comparable to the leadership they have been led to believe exists in other organizational settings, and that institutional progress depends upon the directives of hard-driving, knowledgeable, and decisive executives. This may lead people to see colleges and universities as the long shadows of great leaders, or assert, as James Fisher[4] has done, that "our future rests on the bold, decisive leadership of college and university presidents nationwide." Others disagree. Donald Walker[5] has said that the "view of the university as the shadow of a strong president is unrealistic now, however, if indeed it was ever accurate," and Cohen and March,[6] in their classic *Leadership and Ambiguity*, have gone so far as to say that the "presidency is an illusion."

Calling for leadership is easy, and so everyone does it. But there is still no agreement on how leadership in higher education can be defined, measured, assessed, or linked to outcomes. We do not know how to distinguish leaders from nonleaders, or effective leaders from ineffective ones. The study of leadership in colleges and universities is even more difficult than in other settings because of the unique properties of these organizations. In particular, the relationship between those identified as leaders and those whom they presume to lead is problematic. Some theoretical approaches assert that leadership can be understood only in the context of "followership." But in higher education, there is a strong resistance to leadership as it is generally understood in more traditional and hierarchical organizations. In mature universities it may be more appropriate under most circumstances to think of faculty as constituents rather than as followers.

Identifying faculty as constituents rather than as followers changes the metaphors and symbols that direct our understandings of governance from those of bureaucracy and collegium to those of democratic politics. Concepts such as the consent of the governed, checks and balances of power, and leadership as service become important ways of mediating the tensions between administrative and professional authority. But the implications of the metaphor go further. Unlike a business, in which administrative authority emphasizes opportunities for leadership primarily at the top, the coequal status of professional authority with administrative authority in a university creates opportunities for leadership all through the system. Those who lead on one issue are the constituents on another. Presidents and deans may have a greater obligation than others to set the example and tone, create visions, secure resources and distribute them fairly, and keep operations running smoothly, but the administrative obligation for this kind of leadership is not an exclusive one. *Shared* authority implies *shared* leadership, as well as shared responsibility and accountability.

Organizational leadership is important, but the idea of shared authority suggests that it is a mistake to believe that all leadership must come from formal "leaders." Selznick's[7] classic definition of leadership refers to the ability to infuse daily behavior with meaning, to create an "institutional embodiment of purpose." In a mature university, the responsibility identified by Selznick to "interpret the role and character of the enterprise, to perceive and develop models for thought and behavior, and to find modes of communication that will inculcate general rather than merely partial perspectives" is in large measure fulfilled through the socialization of the participants, professional traditions, and institutional histories, as much as it is by individuals identified as leaders.

A system of shared governance is a system of mutual dependence in which we are all simultaneously leaders and constituents in a process of social exchange. We create our university through our consistent interactions as we work out the reality that leaders are as dependent on constituencies as constituencies are on leaders. Good governance is important for many reasons, but the most obvious is that for each of us it is in our enlightened self-interest.

The Cybernetics of Governance

I have argued, first, that governance is the process of reconciling unique organizational conflicts related to roles and the dual sources of authority in higher education and, second, that leadership in governance is a collective responsibility. The governance systems of most institutions are complex and confusing, authority is fragmented, and patterns of leadership and followership shift by issue and over time. It appears to be a recipe for chaos. And yet, even under the most trying circumstances, students arrive every year, are educated, and graduate. Research is conducted, the results of scholarship are published, community service is performed. Supplies and equipment are purchased, bills are paid, ceremonies are held. Despite the apparent disarray, there is incredible regularity and stability in many aspects of university life. If leadership is so diffused, how is this large and complex social system coordinated?

The third argument is that this coordination is accomplished through cybernetic controls—that is, through self-correcting mechanisms that monitor organizational functions and provide attention cues, or negative feedback, to participants when things are not going well.[8] Systems of negative feedback detect and correct errors, so that when something happens that moves a university in an undesirable direction, something else automatically happens to bring it back on course. Thus, coordination is not provided by one omniscient and rational leader, but by the spontaneous corrective actions of the university's parts.

A thermostat is a simple example of a self-correcting, cybernetic control system with a feedback loop. It turns the furnace on when the environment's temperature falls below a preset limit and turns it off when the temperature returns to the desired level. The thermostat has only one goal: to keep the temperature in an acceptable range. In contrast, a university has not one but a number of goals that must be kept in an acceptable range. If any of them fall outside that range, concerned individuals or groups act like organizational thermostats. Their energies are activated in an attempt to return functioning to an acceptable level. The goals for which such thermostats exist can be things we often talk about, such as the quality of teaching or research, or things we don't talk about but are still real, such as the need to control pollution or to limit workplace accidents. But whether the goals are overt or latent, as long as there is a process through which data concerning them are collected and made available to potential interest groups, there is likely to be some response when the "temperature" gets too high or too low.

A university has many such organizational thermostats, some responsive to explicit administrative controls manifested in organizational rules, regulations, and structures, and others based on implicit professional controls. If the environment was simple, simple governance systems could adequately respond to it. But as environments become complex, governance systems must become equally complex if they are to sense changes and make appropriate adaptations. The different groups and interests within the university allow governance participants to simplify complexity. Each may pay attention to a somewhat different aspect of the environment while ignoring others.

The interaction of these thermostats leads most institutions to function relatively smoothly most of the time. Coordination of their parts is provided primarily by the constraints established at higher organizational levels, by the cultural context in which the subunits interact, and by the training and experience of the various participants. The task of leaders in a cybernetic system, in Clark Kerr's[9] words, is to keep the institution's "lawlessness within reasonable bounds." To do this, cybernetic leaders pay attention to what is wrong. They are concerned with identifying and eliminating weakness and problems, and much of their time is taken up with responding to disturbances in the structure. The machinery of governance runs smoothly most of the time, and in the felicitous expression of my colleague George Keller, leaders listen for the noise in the machine so that they can make adjustments as necessary.

The aphorism that the squeaky wheel gets the grease is not all wrong in a cybernetic university. Leaders assess the cause of the squeak and decide if it is important enough to attend to. Under shared governance there are many leaders, and their different institutional roles bring some squeaks to the attention of one but not others. It is not surprising that different leaders, each seeking to promote a vision of the long-term interest of the institution consistent with the parts of the environment that they see, often have different agendas. It is not these differences that cause problems; rather, it is the difficulty parties sometime have in accepting that the positions held by others represent good faith efforts to resolve what they believe to be important problems. The self-correcting properties of cybernetic systems are constrained when parties ignore or try to smooth over these differences, refuse to recognize the validity of the position of the other, or attempt to dominate the other to achieve their own goals. Good cybernetic governance systems, in contrast, recognize the legitimacy of these different agendas, and parties accept the responsibility for working toward solutions that are mutually satisfactory. This does not mean that each one gets what he or she initially wants, but rather that each one's concerns are accepted as real. Every major administrative problem must become a faculty problem; every important faculty problem must be accepted as something of concern to the administration. A noise in the machine that is not attended to is likely to grow louder until sometimes some important organizational component fails and the institution faces a crisis.

Organizational Processes and Governance in Cybernetic Systems

The fourth argument is that, while all governance systems are ultimately idiosyncratic, their cybernetic properties suggest some simple and general rules about what to do, and what not to do, that can help them evolve.

Cybernetic systems are notoriously difficult to change; the same forces that make them unlikely to fail also make them difficult to improve. And so I will begin with a caution. Attempts to solve governance problems through unilateral activist interventions—regardless of the merits of the new system—are likely to create still more significant problems. Cybernetic social systems are nonlinear and complex, and direct attempts to change them often lead to counterintuitive outcomes. Such efforts may disturb ongoing administrative or professional control systems, and interventions may exacerbate rather than moderate problems.

I suggest that faculty and administrative leadership can improve governance by helping to strengthen their institution's cybernetic capabilities and avoiding drastic actions to impose their own solutions. I praise constraint. Cybernetic leaders follow the physician's ancient creed: *Primum non nocere* (First, do no harm). And cybernetic leaders are modest. Recognizing that they function in organizations whose internal operations are not fully understood, they adopt three laws of the physician:

If it's working, keep doing it.

If it's not working, stop doing it.

If you don't know what to do, don't do anything.

These deceptively simple rules are often difficult to apply in practice, at least in part because leaders are expected to do *something* when things go wrong. But quick fixes, precipitant action, or Gordian knot solutions have limited applications in any organization, and are particularly unlikely to be functional in higher education. Leaders should not do the work of constituencies by fixing things that go wrong in a university; instead, they should provide services that assist constituencies to do their own work and collectively fix it themselves. The most important leadership activities in a university are not making decisions but helping each other make collective sense of what it is we are doing. Cybernetic leaders do this by attending to critical organizational elements such as the availability of information, channels of communication, openness, and forums for interaction.

Consider the importance of information, for example. On many campuses, important data are not collected, or they are collected but only made available selectively, or they are made available but in formats that do not speak to the interests of constituents and therefore never truly become information. Information is the life-blood of an effective cybernetic system, but it does not automatically distribute itself throughout a university. A governance system is clearly in trouble if leaders of various constituencies meet only infrequently with each other, if they seldom communicate important messages to their constituents, if they restrict the free flow of important information, if they deliberately attempt to mislead others, or if they inhibit data comprehension by either distributing too little data or else by distributing enormous amounts of uninterpreted data. Effective governance is more likely to exist when regularized systems report data that campus constituents think is important, when constituents regularly receive information outlining emerging issues and requesting comments and suggestions, when leaders meet regularly in both formal and informal settings with representatives of different constituent groups, and when in other ways the opportunity both to disseminate important information to others on campus and to hear what others have to say is ensured.

If cybernetic monitors are to fulfill their sensing and feedback functions effectively, there must be open access to channels of communication. Lack of information can prevent monitors from receiving negative feedback, and incomplete communication links can prevent them from reporting error to other organizational levels. A concern for information and for creating open communication channels between all organizational components at a level they consider appropriate may be a factor differentiating successful and unsuccessful governance systems.

Good communication is facilitated by a general sense of openness in institutional governance and climate. To be sure, not everything can or should be exposed to public scrutiny, and there are times when secrecy is necessary to protect individual rights or organizational interests. But openness in an academic community should always be the presumption, and secrecy the exception. It is almost certain that disruption is far more likely to be caused by information purposefully or inadvertently kept secret than by sensitive issues inappropriately disclosed. The cybernetic leader can help to influence this by "open plans, open policy statements, open findings, open reasons, open precedents, and fair informal and formal procedures."[10] How "open" is open? How "fair" is fair? There are no rules. It can be only what the constituents agree it is.

Cybernetic leaders, both faculty and administrators, should also be concerned that forums exist in which the various constituencies interested in this information can interact. Some forums may be built into the structure as cabinets, councils, committees, or assemblies; others may be temporarily developed in the form of task forces, ad hoc committees, retreats, or colloquiums to meet specific needs. Forums should help leaders listen for the noise in the machine and enable them to work collectively to reduce it.

Designing the "Best" Governance System

These, then, are my four arguments: governance is an invention to balance legitimate interests, shared governance presumes shared leadership and shared followership, governance systems rely on cybernetic principles to be self-correcting, and cybernetics suggests the value of an emphasis on communicating information and establishing forums for interaction. Do these arguments make sense at a unionized university?

Collective bargaining need not determine the quality of governance. To be sure, unionized campuses have sometimes been the locus of bitter conflict—but such conflict has been seen on non-unionized campuses as well. Research on the relationship of unionization to governance and campus climate suggests that bargaining is more likely to reflect previous campus relationships than it is to create new ones. We have all seen bargaining on some campuses degenerate into brawls whose sole purpose was to defeat the other side. But I have also worked with unionized institutions interested in developing collaborative approaches to bargaining. I can attest to "bargaining sessions" indistinguishable in terms of purpose and process from the best problem-solving committees I have seen on a campus, and to contracts believed by all parties to reflect their best interests.

It is comforting to believe that there is one best way to manage, to lead, or to facilitate governance. But after a lifetime of experience, Clark Kerr[11] wrote,

> I once thought that alternative modes of governance had substantial significance in American higher education. . . . I would now advance the conclusion that, within the range of alternatives considered in the United States, forms of governance make some difference, but not as much as often supposed. . . . One specific arrangement in governance versus another has minor implications for what actually happens in a university.

If there are no models, how can the "goodness" of a governance system be assessed? In my judgment, the acid test of governance in a mature university is not the extent to which various groups are able to exercise influence, but rather the degree to which the system is *acceptable* to the constituents. When it is accepted, processes should run reasonably smoothly according to cybernetic principles. Problems of various kinds should be sensed by one or another organizational unit, and organizational responses should bring the organization back to an acceptable level of functioning. There should be few examples of severe discontinuities in institutional operations.

Where the system is not accepted, levels of satisfaction are likely to be low, the system may become too simple for its environment, problems are not properly attended to, and the institution may appear to lurch from crisis to crisis. People in such systems are likely to spend too much time focusing on their differences instead of discussing their similarities, too much time arguing positions instead of describing problems, and too much time trying to convince others of the justice of their position and too little in trying to understand the justice in the position of others. Governance systems that are not accepted by the parties lead almost inexorably to disruptive conflict.

Governance is not in its essence a structure, but a shared idea about how to do higher education. In the words of the Carnegie Foundation,[12] governance is simply

> the process by which people pursue common ends and, in the process, breathe life into otherwise lifeless forms. The best measure of the health of a governance structure at a college is not how it looks on paper, but the climate in which it functions. Do those involved see some point to what they are doing? Do they believe their efforts can make a difference? Is there a sense of excitement? Is the leadership confident of its aims and goals, without being isolated from either the larger society or the particular institutional community on whose behalf leadership is being exercised?

Good governance doesn't just happen. It requires that participants listen carefully to others' perceptions and problems, with each acknowledging that the concerns of the other are valid and must be attended to. In a mature university, no imposed governance system, regardless of any of its characteristics, can long be good. And no system jointly accepted by experienced professionals who are committed to the survival, integrity, and development of a responsive institution of high academic quality can long be bad.

NOTES

Note: This chapter was prepared pursuant to a grant from the Office of Educational Research and Improvement/Department of Education (OERI/ED). However, the opinions expressed herein do not necessarily reflect the position or policy of the OERI/ED, and no official endorsement by the OERI/ED should be inferred. Portions of this chapter are based upon R. Birnbaum, *How Colleges Work*, San Francisco: Jossey-Bass, 1988.

1. G. Keller, *Academic Strategy* (Baltimore: Johns Hopkins University Press, 1983).

2. T. Veblen, *The Higher Learning in America* (New York: Sagamore Press, 1957; original published in 1918).

3. Joint Statement on Government of Colleges and Universities (1966); *AAUP Policy Documents and Reports* (Washington, D.C.: American Association of University Professors, 1984).

4. J. L. Fisher, *Power of the Presidency* (New York: Macmillan, 1984).

5. D. C. Walker, *The Effective Administrator* (San Francisco: Jossey-Bass, 1979).

6. M. D. Cohen and J. G. March, *Leadership and Ambiguity* (New York: McGraw-Hill, 1974).

7. P. Selznick, *Leadership in Administration* (New York: Harper & Row, 1957).

8. R. Birnbaum, *How Colleges Work* (San Francisco: Jossey-Bass, 1988).

9. C. Kerr, *The Uses of the University* (Cambridge, Mass.: Harvard University Press, 1963).

10. K. P. Mortimer and A. C. Caruso, "The Process of Academic Governance and the Painful Choices of the 1980s," in D. G. Brown (ed.), *Leadership Roles of Chief Academic Officers* (San Francisco: Jossey-Bass, 1984).

11. C. Kerr, "Postscript 1982," *Change* Vol 14, 7 (October 1984): 23–31.

12. Carnegie Foundation for the Advancement of Teaching, *The Control of the Campus* (Washington, D.C.: The Foundation, 1982).

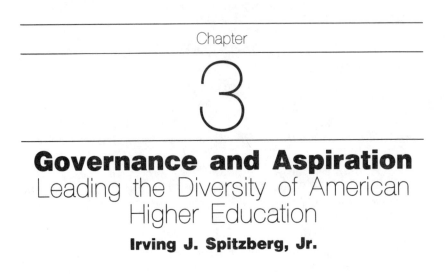

Chapter

3

Governance and Aspiration
Leading the Diversity of American Higher Education
Irving J. Spitzberg, Jr.

To talk about governance in American higher education is to invoke a subject that is generally rhetorical and rarely analytical. Outside of the deliberations of trustees and the complaints of faculty, there is little recent conversation about governance—shared or otherwise—in American higher education. The participation debates of the 1960s faded to campaigns for collective bargaining in the 1970s and then to the management mentality of the 1980s. Only recently have issues of governance reemerged in articulated concern about leadership in American higher education. The conversation has not been about shared governance, except in the pages of faculty publications.

In this chapter, I wish to analyze the diversity of governance in American higher education and the role that leadership plays in a variety of settings. I shall connect these issues of governance and leadership with the way in which different types of institutions accomplish their missions and contribute to quality and equality of opportunity and access in their institutional settings. I shall also examine the connection between aspiration and vision, on the one hand, and governance on the other. Finally, I will argue that the major variable connecting governance structure and aspiration to outcomes of quality or access is the existence or lack thereof of community, which is dependent upon the sense of participation of all constituencies in the governance process.

For the purposes of this essay, I shall talk about governance in terms of the patterns of authority and power on American campuses.

I shall examine the ways in which these patterns interact with institutional aspirations to affect quality and equality. When I invoke authority, I mean informal and formal consent. When I talk about power, I am referring to the influence that comes from position and external support without reference to consent. This distinction between authority and power is essential for understanding the impact of different patterns of governance on quality and equality on American campuses. Only with this distinction at hand can we turn to questions about leadership, which is the process by which groups (in this case, institutions) get their work done through consent in the delegation of authority to act on their behalf and in their interest.

In order to examine governance and leadership, one must always specify context. Although there are general values that ought to inform any discussion of governance—and, from my perspective, those are the values of participation invoked in the language of shared governance—these values must be taken to contexts that vary considerably across the horizon of American colleges and universities.

To illustrate the range of governance approaches in American higher education, I have drawn on two significant samples of case studies, one prepared by the Carnegie Foundation[1] and the other by Bowen and Schuster.[2] The former includes twenty-nine case studies that primarily focus on undergraduate education. The latter includes thirty case studies whose emphasis is the state of the American professoriate. Both sets of case studies contain substantial information on governance and leadership that can be connected with quality and equality—of undergraduate education in the Carnegie study and faculty life in the Bowen and Schuster work. From these, I have created five synthetic cases to illustrate the diversity of governance and cultures and the impact of that diversity on quality and equality. Due to limitations of space, the descriptions and the analysis will be quite conclusionary, but the judgments are based on a very substantial sample of case studies.

I have constructed the following five cases:

1. **Illuminata College**—small, private, church-related college
2. **Normal University**—former public teachers college that grew in the 1960s into a comprehensive university
3. **Flagship University**—the oldest and leading public university in the state

4. Metroplex University—an urban institution, either public or private

5. Elite University—a private research university

All of American higher education—with the exception of community colleges and proprietary education—will be represented by one of these synthetic cases. Some particular campuses, of course, will share features with more than one case. I shall briefly outline the governance structure of each of the cases and connect the campus aspirations for the future of the institution to the dynamics of governance as it affects quality and equality.

1. Illuminata College

Illuminata College has about 1,000 sister institutions.[3] It is a college of no more than 2,000 students and about 100 faculty members. Everyone knows everyone else. It is not selective in its admissions, and its faculty members teach a large number of courses per semester. The president rules the institution, although he (and, for the most part, he *is* a male) must be sensitive to his lay board of trustees and particularly the chair. The institution is quite dependent upon the board for its small endowment and for its annual fund. Ninety-five percent of its income comes from student tuition, so it is dependent upon the student market.

Illuminata has a religious tradition that sets the culture of the institution. The administration is paternalistic, so even though the faculty has little authority outside of the curriculum, the paternalistic decisions are taken with the benefit of intimate knowledge of everyone's views on any issue.

Quality assessment at Illuminata is a matter of judgment about teaching. The quality of teaching at this small, religious institution is completely dependent upon the commitment of the faculty. The fact that faculty even in this small institution do not feel in control of the institution affects their attitude.[4] Most are destined to spend the rest of their careers at Illuminata because they do not engage in research and publication. Since they know they must stay, they devote great energy to teaching and, for the most part, enjoy it. Therefore, the quality of teaching at the institution is often better than the price of the education.

Since admission is open, tuition relatively low, and college finances weak, scholarships are few and not generous. Nevertheless, Illuminata provides an open door to a range of minorities because of the low tuition, although blacks, in particular, are not well represented. There is no policy decision to increase quality of opportunity, but Illuminata is a critical player in the pattern of opportunity in American higher education.

The sharing of governance at Illuminata is in the form of faculty consideration of academic policy matters. The faculty as a whole— it is small enough to meet with everyone attending—considers all academic policy matters, but on matters of budget construction and approval there is only modest faculty input. The chief financial officer and the chair of the board of trustees, which constitute a triumvirate together with the president, decide most major allocation questions. The salary scale is informally negotiated with a faculty committee of elders, but the constraints are set by the triumvirate. Major changes in direction of the college are usually set by the gift of a major donor, sometimes after long solicitation by the president and sometimes out of the blue. Individual faculty take initiatives with great freedom only when they do not cost money.

Administrative leadership at Illuminata is generally exercised through the invocation of both power and status conferred by the trustees, although over time, when the president and other administrators have been in office for a number of years, the leadership evolves into an activity based on consent of most constituencies and judged by the overall accomplishment of the institution. Faculty leadership usually comes from the elders and seldom is the source of innovation and initiative. Trustee leadership is often vested in a chair who wields great power although having no authority other than the legal rights granted by law.

The governance process has little positive impact on quality and no impact on increased educational opportunity. Institutional quality derives more from the efforts of the faculty as individuals than from a community decision. The aspiration of the college is survival, and it always seems at risk, even in good times. If times are good, tomorrow is likely to be bad. If times are bad, tomorrow is likely to be worse. The feeling of marginality is omnipresent. Campus governance generally has only negative impact, insofar as the process makes the faculty feel alienated and disenfranchised. Only at rare moments in history—during crisis—do all the members of the

Illuminata polity feel that they are part of a community, which is the condition for shared governance and for the accomplishment of quality and equality.

2. Normal University

For decades teachers colleges in the United States have played an important role, both for the public school system and for access to higher education, by providing essentially open-admission, four-year higher education at a low cost. In the 1960s, however, most teachers colleges became general purpose state colleges and universities with uniform aspirations to become like the land-grant flagship in the state. Teacher training, though still substantial, no longer was the keystone of self-image for the institution.[5]

Normal University, like most of its peers, is governed by a distant systems board, with state mandarins and extensive rules and politics. A president and an unusually large administrative bureaucracy for a relatively small public institution—fewer than 10,000 students and about 500 faculty—make major campus decisions. There are two classes of professionals in the institution: faculty and administrators. The former teach, although many wish that they were at a research university; the latter administer. The relationship between administrators and faculty is quite hierarchical: deans and other bureaucrats tell faculty what to do, why their salary is so low, and why they are five to an office.

The top item on the agenda of Normal University is to forget that it once was a teachers college (or an "ag" or "tech" school in some other cases) and to get funding equivalent to Flagship U so that its faculty can do research and so that they can aspire to something more than tugboat status. Improved College Board scores of students at admission and a reduced course load for faculty are taken as the measures of quality improvement. Some modest outside research funding will be the measure of graduation to the top of the minor leagues. The right to offer one or two doctorates is highly coveted. The agenda rarely includes any commitment to teaching, even though teaching is the bread and butter of the institution.

Normal University, like Illuminata, provides a point of entry into American higher education for those who are new to the system and who have little money. Once again, this is not a commitment of the campus but a fact of the diversity of American higher education.

The governance process seldom deals with either quality or access, because both are viewed as determined by systems structure with very little control on campus. The campus president is, in fact, quite powerful, but in reality he is involved with systems politics as part of his daily routine. Other administrators have power as well, but they have little authority because their constituents have not put them in their positions, and they are accountable only to more senior administrators. The faculty are, and perceive themselves to be, employees confronting a hierarchical bureaucracy that treats them as a necessary evil. There is little, if any, shared governance at Normal University.

Patterns of leadership at Normal University appear to be following a script written by Max Weber for larger bureaucracies, even when individual campuses are often rather small. The bureaucracies, however, operate in a complex political system in which some of the most important decisions are out of the hands of those most affected by them. This means that governance is often shared through conflict resolution—on many campuses through adversarial collective bargaining—which makes all of the individuals in the system feel completely disempowered. Leadership of the disempowered, whether by administrators, faculty, or distant systems trustees, seldom seems to contribute to the creation of quality or access. Since consensual authority is generally lacking, the very structure of governance as bureaucracy disconnects governance and leadership from the creation of community. Once again like Illuminata, Normal University's contribution to equality of access comes from its place in the universe of American higher education, not from a self-conscious decision of the polity. Few if any decisions are made about quality, because there is not sufficient community to make collegial judgments. The "leaders by anointment" make any such decisions, and they avoid most such judgments because they create political grief.

3. Flagship University

The current realities of American higher education are defined by Flagship University. In each state such institutions dominate the educational landscape. They are, for the most part, well-funded but never funded well enough to meet their own aspirations. Their expectations set the tone of their states. All fifty states have institutions that aspire to rank in the top ten of land-grant campuses (institutions receiving funds under the Morrill Act of 1862) and/ or flagship institutions in the United States. Only the ten presently there—including, for example, on everyone's list, Berkeley, Michigan, the University of Wisconsin–Madison, and the University of North Carolina–Chapel Hill—have any real hope of being there. But all of the rest covet such rank and are allocating their vision, their energy, and their resources to this task.[6]

Flagship University is governed by a large bureaucracy over which the board or the president exercise little control. Some presidents, at certain times in history, do make a difference. Often they make that difference by moving from the flagship to the system. Clark Kerr, who as Berkeley's president built Berkeley into a world-class institution, moved on to create the modern University of California system. William Friday, who continued the construction of Chapel Hill, subsequently initiated the University of North Carolina system. Typically and for the most part, however, Flagship University operates as a complex bureaucracy in which governance is weak, inertia strong, and leadership responsible to state politics not based on authority vested by constituents in the institution.

The exceptions to this rule are Berkeley and Chapel Hill, and, to a lesser degree, Michigan and Illinois, where a culture of strong faculty control has emerged with equal commitment and interest from alumni as expressed through trustees. These exceptions grew in states where quality was and is supported by state legislatures and governors with confidence in the lay boards; the boards, in turn, delegated much power and authority to campus presidents in partnership with faculty. Members of the legislature, alumni, lay boards, and campus constituencies created alliances to support the campus over many decades, and all feel a stake in the institution. All consent to the exercise of authority because they all feel part of the community of the campus, even when they live far away and participate by voting.

The competitive aspiration of Flagship to Berkeley status has affected resource allocation and commitments to quality and equality. Quality is viewed strictly in terms of research quantity and sponsored research dollars. Students are viewed as fodder for the FTE mill (that is, for cost accounting that divides the number of students taught by the full-time equivalent of faculty), although their College Board scores are relevant to prestige. On all of these campuses the commitment of the upper administrators and a core of senior faculty to the top ten sweepstakes creates a culture of agreement that ties together a system that is quite centrifugal in its dynamic. The top ten have achieved quality because of a collegium connecting faculty, students, administration, alumni, and legislature. Very few of these forty other campuses have understood the model of collegial governance that has characterized Berkeley and Chapel Hill, and earlier Michigan and Madison.

The value of access is lost at Flagship University. The president is committed to raising College Board scores and the faculty want better students. This means that equality of access has been assigned to other institutions as a priority. Meritocracy is the rule of Flagship University, and little effort and few resources are allocated by the governance process to the task of discovering merit outside of the usual populations.

The governance process is quite atomized. The board and the president make global resource allocation decisions. The faculty senate deals with curriculum but only rarely attempts to deal with the details and the overall structure. Quality judgments are left to departments, and the major work of the university—research—is an individual area of activity where even the department is marginal. Quality in research is the interaction of individual scholars with the disciplinary collegium that knows no institutional boundary.

Flagship University views this issue of research quality as most important; here the governance process seldom intervenes. The search for research greatness is the cultural norm. All decisions in the governance process are taken in that cultural context and never challenge it.

Leadership in Flagship University is always overtly political in that the administration is always looking to the state capital to assess every move. The political economy of the university determines the accountability of the leaders to the governor and the legislature, since the fiscal piper calls the institutional tune. However, the research culture sets constraints on interference and itself guarantees some autonomy of leadership. This autonomy is seldom enhanced by administrative leadership because of the personal involvement of the president and senior administrators in the state political process. Faculty leadership seldom contributes to the creation of autonomous community, since the faculty identify with disciplinary departments rather than the campus. Departmental chairs and research stars are the faculty leaders. Faculty senate activists are generally viewed by their peers as engaging in the dirty work of the institution since they cannot be accomplished scholars. One leads because he cannot research; one might teach only because he can neither research nor teach. Very little leadership at Flagship University is based upon the active consent of the governed. Therefore, community leadership contributes little to equality of access or quality: the former is ignored; the latter emerges in research because of the institutional culture but is lost in teaching for the very same reason.

4. Metroplex University

A new type of university has emerged in the United States since the 1960s: the urban institution with a metropolitan sweep. There is a long history of urban institutions in the United States that have become national and world-class institutions—Columbia and Chicago come to mind. During the 1970s and 1980s, however, urban institutions that serve complex constituencies in metropolitan areas have become major actors and points of entry into higher education for minorities, as well as for urban agencies and corporations that need to connect to the knowledge system. Metroplex University is a new institution meeting old needs that have been neglected by the Flagship Universities or which other institutions have been unable to meet.[7]

Metroplex is governed by a local board. Whether it is public or private, the board is dominated by the burghers of the local economic and political system. The president of Metroplex is a political leader who happens to be appointed by a board. He—and now, she, in some significant cases such as Queens College and the University of Missouri–St. Louis—maintains his position by cutting deals between and among campus and off-campus constituencies. He garners resources like a pickpocket, finding money wherever he can.

The quality of life at Metroplex is substandard by any measure. The physical plant is tawdry. It is overcrowded. There are few amenities. There is no sense of community. The faculty are workers. The students are the lumpen proletariat. There is life and activity at all hours of every weekday, but it is a ghost town in the heart of the city during weekends.

Although the quality of life is miserable, the quality of the institution as measured by its graduates and the performance of its faculty is beyond even the most generous expectation. The Hobbesian world of individuals pursuing their own goals without a polity seems to allow performance by the few that affects the many. Policy, however, does not create this quality; indeed, every policy decision at every level creates an impediment. Yet student accomplishment and faculty performance often match those at much wealthier and more coherent institutions.

The quality of opportunities available means that Metroplex contributes to access in very important ways. There is access not only to undergraduate opportunities but also to the full range of graduate and professional schools. Indeed, the internal politics of Metroplex is dominated by professional schools such as law, medicine, business, and engineering. At many large institutions—for example, Flagship University—the professional schools are powerful, but they have special clout at Metroplex, since Metroplex grew out of a confederation of professional units. The creative arts and the liberal arts thrive in islands, if not across the ocean. Quality of access for those who are motivated and seek is quite high at Metroplex. Once again, this is the result of Metroplex's place in the overall structure of higher education as much as the institution's commitment to access.

Leadership in Metroplex follows the model of realpolitik of Talleyrand and Kissinger: the construction of shifting alliances to deal with the conflict or crisis at hand. Administrative leaders can seldom exercise fiat but must cut deals with their peers, faculties, political trustees, the mayor, and diverse interest groups in the metropolitan area. In regard to any particular decision, there is actually a delegation of authority to get something done. But leaders are always looking over their shoulders to watch for assassins of authority and spend much of their energy protecting their blind sides. Faculty leadership is divided between The Faculty and The Union. Internecine warfare among faculty political groupies makes representation more often self-selected activists than persons who emerge with the authority vested by the faculty. There is little substantial alumni leadership, since the alumni are as fragmented as their urban constituency.

The rhetoric of aspiration at Metroplex is quite similar to that at Flagship. Indeed, public urban institutions have become major competitors with flagship institutions for funds. Because of the great diversity of students and faculty at Metroplex, there are more organized political forces affecting the life of the campus, and therefore there may be more islands of quality in this diversity than on most Flagship campuses. It is the informal governance process, not the fact that formal governance is any more collegial, that permits whatever quality we find. Indeed, because of the atomism of the Metroplex society, there is less of a collegium than at the worst of the Flagships. Since many of these urban institutions engage in collective bargaining, there is a culture of adversarial relationship that is the antithesis of a collegium. This adversarial interaction often threatens the very quality that is the essence of the freedom of Metroplex. But the cultural diversity protects quality, and shared institutional commitment to access reduces the tradeoffs at Metroplex so that the inability of the bureaucracy to create community is less damaging than at other institutions.

5. Elite University

The standards of quality in American higher education are set by Elite University and its peer institutions.[8] Here research is king, but a by-product of research quality is outstanding teaching as well. The teaching is a response to the best and the brightest who vie for admission to Elite: only four out of ten of the original applicants are finally admitted.

The Elite is organized along departmental lines, with the departments dominated by the graduate arts and sciences. The undergraduate college is a separate administrative organization, but its teachers are drawn from the confederation of graduate departments in a faculty of arts and sciences. Most of Elite's outstanding faculty wish to teach in the college because its students are even better than the high-quality graduate students admitted to the Ph.D. programs. The patterns of the College of Elite University, in that their faculty—though they view themselves as committed to quality teaching—generally engage in substantial research as well; that research, moreover, is expected of them by their colleagues and their students.

The academic life of Elite is governed by the faculty. Although in theory the president and trustees have roles, they would never interfere in the academic life of the institution. Deans at Elite are much stronger than elsewhere, because they are the point of connection between faculty and administration and because they raise much of the money (Elite operates on the principle that each tub will float on its own bottom). Alumni are important sources of energy and initiative through their financial donations, which are the lifeblood of the institution.

The trustees are mainly large donors, whose only additional task is to select the president. Consultation in governance varies in terms of its formality at Elite, but the informal reality is that no major decision will be taken unless there is substantial consensus across constituencies of faculty, administration, trustees, and alumni. Even students have their say, although they do not have the veto the others have.

Governance at Elite takes place in an environment where everyone shares a sense of community that cuts across constituencies and, indeed, connects generations. Elite is the only institution in the galaxy of American higher education in which the governance process actually addresses quality and access. By contributing to a shared community the governance process can actually set priorities that affect the constituencies of the community to some degree. This authority requires the consent of shared values that seems to be missing in the rest of higher education.[9]

Elite has some economic and much disciplinary diversity but connects its constituencies through the sense of election according to the principles of the meritocracy. There is a very real sense that everyone deserves to be there and therefore should have a role in decisions. And there is an understanding of intergenerational responsibility that reinforces the present community. This combination of culture and structure allows both quality and equality to be taken seriously.

Conclusions

This *tour d'horizon* does not provide a definitive picture of the connection between governance and quality and equality of access or the impact of aspiration on both, but it does suggest the issues that American higher education must address. Although the diversity of reality that these synthetic cases portray does not allow any single recommendation, it does offer five themes that cut across the spectrum of difference.

The first theme is the impact of community on authority and leadership and the resultant ability of the governance process to address issues of quality and access. Without a minimum sense of community, there is no polity. The central point of Alan Bloom's recent diatribe against students[10] is the atomism of American universities. I believe that his argument is relevant everywhere but where he directs it: that is, to the elite institutions. The atomism and lack of community on most other campuses mean that they cannot address the issues of priority in regard to quality and access, particularly with reference to the trade-offs between them that are the essence of judgment. Bloom further claims that the lack of community has led to a moral relativism that makes shared values impossible, or perhaps the moral relativism has led to the lack of community; he is not clear on this point.

The fact that many constituencies on most campuses feel disenfranchised means that the judgments of the policy process seldom appear authoritative. The constituents perceive them as dictates, not agreements. The absence of shared values means that the lack of apparently fair and responsive procedures becomes even more damaging. Both the Carnegie and Bowen and Schuster data and case studies made clear that faculty particularly feel alienated from their communities, except at elite institutions. There, issues of quality and access are explicitly addressed by the constituencies, because only there is there a polity to address them. It is only at these institutions—and to a lesser degree and in a different environment, at Metroplex—that leaders feel obligated to take seriously all of the constituencies—faculty, alumni, trustees, and students. And only at Elite and Illuminata do all of the constituencies play a role at different times.

A second theme is the way in which the national system does allow for both quality and access, although not usually at the same place. Taken as a whole, the American system of higher education seems to address access almost completely in structural terms. Illuminata College and Normal University provide access because they are low on the status ladder and their structural position requires open admission. Illuminata's tuition may be a barrier, but many of these private institutions have relatively low costs, and federal loans are available to the lowest income students to cover these low-status-campus costs. Flagship University is not required structurally to address access issues, so it doesn't. (I should, however, note that in important states—for example, Texas, California, Florida, and New York—the growing political power of minorities, who want both the status and the achievement of meeting the standards of Flagship, will remove the structural protection for Flagship and use external power to force changes.) Elite University actually addresses the problem, because it is a community that can set priorities. Yet its culture severely limits the contribution it can make to access, since it is the institutionalization of meritocracy. The socioeconomic realities make it unlikely that pure meritocracy will actually provide equality of opportunity.

The priority of access depends upon the accountability of leaders on campus to constituencies off campus. Public institutions that must respond to legislatures may in the future be the most likely to make access a priority, but even then it will seldom be the choice of the campus itself.

The ability to address quality questions is also limited structurally, which provides a third theme. Illuminata will never offer learning opportunities in a range of fields at the level of sophistication of Elite University. Nor will it easily establish qualitative standards appropriate to its structural position, because those standards are actually set by Elite and Flagship. But with attention to the creation of communities, it is possible for an Illuminata and a Normal to set their own standards and distinguish their own aspirations. The idiosyncratic colleges such as Hampshire, Reed, Antioch, and St. John's have for decades been marching to their own drummers. Their commitments to visions unique to their institutions and justified to the larger world established a community of interest. Northeast Missouri State, too, has broken the lockstep of the marching orders with leadership and a community of support. The condition for addressing issues of quality is a combination of institutional mechanisms for creating a polity and leadership toward a set of shared values that can be distinguished from but justified by the norms of the larger universe of higher education.

Those who have bemoaned the present and looked back to some golden age of community and standards—Allan Bloom, William Bennett, and others—have understood that the breakdown of community has affected quality in American higher education and identified a fourth important theme. What they have missed is that this breakdown has flowed from unresponsive governance systems as much as from the erosion of a long-lost common culture. The

AAUP 1966 *Joint Statement on Government of Colleges and Universities*[11] nicely summarizes an ideal of shared governance that is seldom invoked, much less implemented. Of course, the ideal model will even be broader in that it will include alumni and students in its sweep.

Our challenge is to create governance institutions that allow some minimum agreement about core institutional values, while protecting diversity and acknowledging that compromise is necessary for communities to set priorities. An aspiration of all public institutions becoming Flagship Universities, all Flagship Universities becoming Berkeleys, and all privates becoming either Harvards or Radcliffes is an impossible dream, one that will lead to the nightmare of frustration and erosion of quality that one sees in Flagships, Normals, and some Illuminatas around the country—and that make Don Quixote look like a Trumanesque realist. Cultures that acknowledge values of quality *and* access and then create governance systems with the authority necessary to set priorities can operate in a system of diversity and provide real opportunity to achieve both.

Finally, the Illuminatas, Normals, Flagships, Metroplexes, and Elites all have their place in the system in a way that gives the whole both diverse quality and access. No one campus type, by itself, can meet the needs of the system. All need to commit themselves to the search for community as the basis of both access and quality. There will be trade-offs between the two, but there can be no effective decisions without the minimum agreement about goals necessary to govern. The strength of the American system is that its structure virtually guarantees access to higher education; its weakness, and a necessary one, is that quality is variable. The task is to recognize diverse sorts of quality for different students and institutions, but not to use diversity to mask poor quality in the pursuit of a variety of goals.

The collegium requires attention to and a balance between aspiration and reality that American higher education seldom achieves but that other national systems accomplish even more rarely. This balance directly depends upon leadership and access to leadership for those who understand that they are accountable to constituents both on campus and off, to this generation and generations to come. Bemoaning the present in comparison with an idyllic past will not lead to the future; only modesty and an agreement to seek shared futures will actually forge aspirations that transform realities.

NOTES

1. Background studies prepared for Ernest L. Boyer, *College: The Undergraduate Experience in America* (New York: Harper and Row, 1987).

2. Howard Bowen and Jack Schuster, *The American Professoriate* (New York: Oxford University Press, 1986).

3. In regard to Illuminata and each of the subsequent synthetic cases, I shall identify the campuses in the two sets of case data that provide the basis of the synthesis. In regard to the Carnegie data, I shall provide only the code names used in the internal documents. I shall cite particular campuses from the Bowen and Schuster list, since they published the complete list of campuses. In addition, I will note any other campuses on which I have notes drawn from visits over the last eight years, in addition to those listed in the other studies, most of which I have visited as well.

Carnegie campuses: Altamont College, Boone College, Crimson College, Faith College, Landon University, Larousse College, Masson College, Pulaski Institute for the Liberal Arts, Roger Mayne University, Southern Christian College.

Bowen and Schuster: University of the Pacific, Hills College, Alma College, Morehouse College, Saint Mary's College.

Personal Visits: Philander Smith College, Hanover College, University of Tampa.

4. A recent study by Professor Eugene R. Rice and Ann H. Austin, "High Morale and Satisfaction Among Faculty: Ten Exceptional Colleges," *Change Magazine*, xx, 2 (March/April, 1988), pp. 14–15, indicated that faculty on campuses such as Illuminata are happier than most places, in part because they feel more in control of the circumstances directly affecting their performance, and feel more a part of their campus community than colleagues on other campuses. This positive feeling exists in spite of the fact that faculty in these institutions are more poorly paid than colleagues on other and larger campuses. The Rice and Austin data are more encouraging than the Carnegie and Bowen/Schuster data but are consistent with the general pattern.

5. Carnegie: East State University, North Kingston University, Northwestern Research University, Prudential College, Rolling Rock University, Southwest Technical University, Western State A&M.

Bowen and Schuster: Cal State–LA, Northern Arizona University, Southern Connecticut State University, Jersey City State College, Southern University–New Orleans.

Personal Visits: Georgia State University, Central Connecticut State University, Cal State–Sacramento, Cal State–San Diego, Cal State–Hayward, SUNY/Brockport, SUNY/Fredonia, SUNY/College at Buffalo, Kent State

University, Southern Illinois University, South Florida University, George Mason University, Bowie State University.

6. Carnegie: Eberhardt University, University of the Southwest, Yonnodio University.

Bowen and Schuster: University of California–Berkeley, University of Iowa, University of Michigan–Ann Arbor, University of New Mexico, Washington State University, University of Nevada–Reno.

Personal Visits: University of North Carolina–Chapel Hill, North Carolina State, University of Connecticut–Storrs, University of Maryland–College Park, University of California–Los Angeles, University of Colorado–Boulder, University of Mississippi–Oxford, University of Massachusetts–Amherst, Rutgers, University of Arkansas–Fayetteville, University of Texas–Austin, University of Wisconsin–Madison, Florida State University, University of Minnesota–Minneapolis/St. Paul, University of Indiana–Bloomington, University of West Virginia, Ohio State.

7. Carnegie: All Saints University, Ashby University, New England State University, Urban University.

Bowen and Schuster: New York University, University of Louisville, Fordham University, University of Denver, University of Alabama–Birmingham, University of Hartford.

Personal Visits: University of Missouri–St. Louis, CUNY/City College, CUNY Graduate Center, SUNY/Buffalo, University of Texas–Dallas, University of Miami.

8. Carnegie: Crossley College for Women, Marlowe University, Yardley University.

Bowen and Schuster: University of Pennsylvania, Tulane University, Colorado College, Grinnell College, Swarthmore College.

Personal Visits: Columbia, Harvard, Yale, Princeton, Brown, MIT, Cal Tech, Amherst, Stanford, University of Chicago.

9. There are other exceptions—e.g., the Elite small liberal arts colleges, special characteristic colleges such as Reed and St. John's, and the Elite flagships such as Berkeley and Chapel Hill. But for the most part, only the Elite universities have been able to build the community that is the condition of governance having impact on quality and access.

10. Allan Bloom, *The Closing of the American Mind* (New York: Simon and Schuster, 1987).

11. *AAUP Policy Documents and Reports* (The Redbook) (Washington, D.C., 1984), p. 105.

Principals and Agents in Campus Governance

Kathryn Mohrman

Elizabeth Arnold glanced through the stack of telephone messages, student papers, and campus mail that had accumulated during the previous week while she was giving a paper at the American Association for the Advancement of Science. The pile included the agenda for the department meeting at noon today (*Will we ever stop talking about candidates and actually hire someone for that assistant professor slot?*), the usual requests for letters of recommendation (*At least I'll have a break from medical school letters with Michael's applications for graduate programs in public policy*), a note from one of the graduate assistants in the lab (*She may have found an interesting new approach to the problem that has been giving us so much trouble*), a letter from the dean of arts and sciences (*Oh, no, not another request for committee service!*), mass mailings from the central administration on campus and from a range of professional organizations nationally. The telephone messages were also varied, although the most intriguing one was from a program officer at the National Institutes of Health (*If they are asking me for clarification on a section of my proposal, they must be interested in my new project*). She headed down the hall to her office, where she found a number of late papers from students shoved under her office door; she put the whole pile on her desk and tried to decide what to tackle first (*Why do so many people have claims on my time?*). Elizabeth Arnold began another week as a biology professor at Northern University.

James Adams looked at a similar accumulation in his office in the Political Science Department at Central University in another state, although his pile was larger because he serves on the campus appointment, promotion, and tenure committee this year (*Another eight folders to read before Wednesday, and these are thick ones*). He quickly ripped open the envelope with the governor's seal on it (*Well, well, an invitation to serve on a state commission on regional economic development; about time the governor realized that this part of the state needs some attention*), then turned to the urgent note from the department chair about next semester's schedule (*John and I will have that new course ready to go by fall*), two requests for reprints of the article he published last year (*People are finally reading it*), and an announcement from the university's president that Central had been ranked favorably in a recent national poll on higher education (*Our efforts to improve our quality may be starting to pay off at long last*). He had a class in ten minutes, so all of these matters needing attention would have to wait (*Why do so many people have claims on my time?*).

Elizabeth Arnold, James Adams, and their counterparts at colleges and universities across the country work in a complex environment of multiple demands and multiple goals. They find themselves in a web of relationships on campus with colleagues in their own departments, on committees, with senior administrators, with non-academic officers of the institution; they have a similar network off-campus with faculty in their own disciplines at other institutions and in national associations, with policymakers in community organizations and state government, and with program officials in federal agencies that sponsor academic research. This chapter looks at these relationships through the lens of principal-agent analysis in order to understand better the structures and decision-making processes of higher education.

These relationships vary widely by the discipline of the faculty member involved, by the size of the campus, its sources of funding, its primary mission, the nature of its student body, and other factors. The autonomy of the research professor at a prestigious land-grant university is quite different from the requirements placed on a young faculty member teaching commuting students at an open door–admissions college. Yet they share certain traits, among them a commitment to academic values, a desire for collegiality, and a responsibility to many players inside and outside the institution. As this chapter shows, higher education differs from many other organizations in American society because professors have substantial authority even though they reside nominally at the bottom of the academic hierarchy; the concept of "coupled dependency" describes a relationship in which faculty members can be both principals and agents with the deans, government bureaucrats, and colleagues with whom they work. This paper ends with an analysis of the implications for campus governance of these special qualities of academic life.

The Essentials of Agency

The world is a web of principal-agent relationships. Individuals in business enterprises, government bureaucracies, and colleges and universities are linked in relationships of mutual dependency. An agency relationship exists whenever one individual (the principal) depends upon the actions of another (the agent) to achieve the principal's goals; the dilemma is one of control of subordinates through inducements and sanctions to get them to work toward the principal's objectives rather than their own when goals are in conflict.[1] In a whole series of principal-agent relationships—employer-employee, client-lawyer, investor-broker, citizen-politician— the principal contracts with the agent in order to achieve the principal's goals, yet the agent is not necessarily motivated to act on behalf of the principal rather than to pursue his own self-interest. The success of the principal-agent relationship depends in large part on the creation of an incentive and monitoring structure that produces results as close as possible to the optimal.

Principals and agents suffer from information asymmetries; agents know more about their own tasks, but principals usually know more about the goals to be accomplished. Useful information is imperfectly available and costly to obtain on both sides. Given these problems, no organization can function as well as it would if all information were costlessly shared and if incentives between principals and agents could be costlessly aligned. Instead, there will inevitably be some discrepancy between desired and actual performance. Such agency costs depend upon the degree to which the principal can truly observe her agent's behavior, the environmental constraints that limit monitoring and rewards, and the degree of congruence of interest between parties in the relationship.

In higher education, the major form of agency relationship is that of employer-employee, so the academic workplace illustrates some of the fundamental characteristics of principals and agents. Before an offer is made, the employer wants to learn as much as possible about the abilities of a job applicant, but ultimately she cannot discern the applicant's values, attitudes, and intellect. In addition, it is not in the self-interest of the applicant to reveal true information, for overstatement of his capabilities may enhance his chances of obtaining the desired position. At the same time, he wants to know more about job conditions than the employer is often willing or able to reveal.[2]

Once the worker has been hired, the problems of asymmetric information do not disappear. The principal cannot determine the true productivity of each agent, so she often relies on proxy measures for behavior that contributes to her goals. In addition, in most employment situations the final output is a joint product of many workers, so it is difficult if not impossible to determine the precise contribution of each employee to that output. This combination of common product and costly monitoring encourages shirking, because the benefit of slacking off accrues completely to the lazy worker, while the costs of lower productivity are borne by the entire work team.

These basic themes in principal-agent theory—mutual dependency, asymmetric information, shirking, and the necessity of incentives and monitoring—were first developed in economics to explain relationships in the profit-making firm when some of the assumptions of neoclassical economics were relaxed. Recently such concepts have been applied to public bureaucracies and political institutions[3] to investigate such issues as hierarchy, control, and accountability outside of market structures.

This chapter examines the ways in which principals and agents function in higher education. In an enterprise that lacks the incentives of profit that exist in business and the sanctions of government that exist in bureaucracies, how are intellectual and educational goals achieved? Do principals and agents behave differently in higher education than in other types of organizations? What explanatory power does the concept have for understanding academic governance?

Although the specifics of principal-agent relationships vary widely from one campus to another, the focus here is on research universities because the importance of federal support for graduate training and research adds an extra level of complexity to the decision-making process on such campuses. The examination of faculty roles concentrates on those individuals who have direct responsibility for carrying out the institution's tripartite mission of teaching, research, and service. The analysis focuses on the professor in his agent relationship with principals both outside and inside the university, including state government officials, community representatives, and especially program officers in the National Science Foundation (NSF), the National Institutes of Health (NIH), and other federal research agencies, as well as deans, presidents, and other administrators on campus. Questions of governance are more tangled—and also more interesting—because of these external principals. While faculty on many campuses do not interact with such a wide range of external constituents, an examination of principals and agents in complex institutions is useful for several reasons: the prestige of such institutions suggests that others are likely to imitate them, and the nature of academic work, plus the authority of knowledge possessed by faculty members, brings principals and agents together in unique ways that illuminate both academic governance and principal-agent theory.

Principals and Agents Inside the University

Higher education serves multiple goals in modern society, so it is no surprise that professors have multiple principals on their own campuses. Department chairs, deans, provosts, and presidents are principals providing incentives and sanctions for their faculty agents to produce more scholarly output, to bring bigger enrollments to the department, to increase institutional visibility and prestige, to recruit the best prospects as junior faculty, and to bring in research grants with their attendant equipment, salary support, and indirect costs. At times, the same person can represent more than one objective, as in the case of the dean who talks with her faculty agents about both research productivity and improved teaching effectiveness. At different universities, priorities shift among the discovery of new knowledge, its transmission to the next generation, and its application to public problems; for different individuals the balance changes in comparison with peers and over time. But on most campuses, faculty are expected to direct their energies in some combination to all three missions. In contrast, then, to the typical businesses in which success is ultimately measured by contributions to profitability, the multiple purposes of the university mean that no single standard of success prevails.

In the firm producing tangible output, the value of which is measured by its market price, the employer's problem is to measure each worker's contribution to that final product.[4] The tasks of the faculty member semester by semester are often solitary, so at first the problems of measurement in higher education seem relatively easy. The principal does not have the joint product dilemma when she can look separately at a course taught by Professor Smith or an article written by Professor Jones. But when one aggregates these activities in thinking about final product in the institutional sense—a high-quality liberal arts education or enhanced prestige for the university—the principal's problem deepens. In undergraduate studies, to take one example, what are the desired results? Is the university imparting occupational skills, a love of learning, analytical ability, preparation for citizenship, loyalty to the institution, or all of the above and more? How does a college measure student achievement of any of these goals? How does one measure the productivity of the individual faculty member, not only in a given semester but as a contributing factor in a student's total baccalaureate experience?

The problem is exacerbated by variations in information and measurement for the different missions of the university, so principals vary in their emphasis on inputs and outputs of the educational process, depending upon the part of the enterprise they are most interested in influencing. Employers often resolve the dilemma of asymmetric information by looking at proxy measures of desired but unobservable qualities. In a business the actual contribution of each worker cannot be measured easily, but the final product has a clear market value. Thus, the employer often uses proxy measures for the actual productivity she cannot determine; wages are based upon such factors as diligence, hours worked, or written reports.

In higher education as well, proxies often substitute for more direct measures of productivity. In teaching, where the result is very difficult to determine even if the objective could be agreed upon, both principal and agent bargain over inputs—teaching load, office hours, FTE (the generation of credit hours) and the like. The real goal of quality instruction, of long-term impact on student learning, may or may not be related to these more accessible input factors. The fact that students are both inputs and outputs in the educational process only complicates an already difficult measurement problem.

In research, output is clearer and input is harder to assess. Deans, faculty committees, and colleagues can look at articles published and even make some qualitative judgments about the results, in addition to making quantitative assessments. What they cannot determine is the quality of effort that went into that research or the number of hours the principal investigator spent on the project. How can they monitor the flash of inspiration that might have come while he was brushing his teeth? Principals, then, are likely to focus on either inputs or outputs, depending upon the ease of measurement in the area of concern, but even so they focus on individual indicators rather than actual assessments of progress toward the institution's multiple goals.[5]

Principals and Agents Outside the University

The research professor in the sciences is agent to the program officer at the National Science Foundation or the Department of Energy at the same time that he is agent to administrators on his own campus; if he has more than one grant, he has several principals outside the university. At the same time, science bureaucrats have other agents on the same campus or among disciplinary colleagues at other universities. The existence of multiple principals and agents suggests competition for research dollars, for the best faculty, for tenure, for higher appropriations for the agency, for prestige, and so on.

The program officer at the Naval Research Laboratory or the Department of Agriculture represents the interests of the citizens of the United States in the development of quieter submarines or more productive strains of wheat. The bureaucrat has the principal's dilemma of possessing incomplete information on the true qualities of grant applicants, but the problem is exacerbated by the nature of scientific inquiry. Especially in basic research, the goal cannot be specified in detail so that the grant is really an agreement to spend a certain level of effort in thinking about a problem. The role of the federal bureaucrat is to support research that will contribute significantly to the field and to the mission of the agency, that is, research conducted by individuals with the intellectual capacity and the facilities to produce sound results.

The principal's task of evaluating research proposals is more difficult than the dilemma of the employer looking at job applications, because the results of the research will depend upon the scholar's ingenuity and creativity as well as more tangible inputs such as equipment and technicians. Not only does the principal suffer from incomplete information, but the agent himself cannot predict with certainty if he will be able to achieve substantial intellectual progress while working on the project; the agent does not have perfect knowledge of his own capabilities, as is the case in other principal-agent relationships. Applied research is no less dependent upon creativity and insight, although the objective of the grant is often more focused since the problem to be addressed is more clearly specified at the outset. Thus, the granting agency may have an easier time evaluating proposals when the purpose of the grant resembles a procurement contract with clear output (buying services to develop more effective solar energy devices, for example) than if it supports basic research in which results are less predictable (studying the molecular properties of cells).

The science bureaucrat is a powerful principal in higher education because of the importance of federal funds for the research effort. While scholars in many areas of the humanities and social sciences work independently, with their largest investment being their own time, faculty in the sciences often cannot undertake significant research at all without external support. The federal government as external principal provides powerful incentives for faculty agents on campus to conduct research that contributes to the national interest in health, basic science, technology, and other fields.

External principals are not limited, however, to program officers in federal agencies. In public universities in particular, state officials are at least as important because they represent the largest block of operating income for the institution. Here the agency relationship operates at the top levels of campus administration more frequently than with individual faculty members; the president of the university is directly linked with the governor and legislature in policy and fiscal determinations. These state officials regularly exercise the functions of principals, including incentives, sanctions, and monitoring, over the university in attempts to shape campus behavior to match state objectives. At the same time, however, faculty and administrators often have substantial authority to present a budget and its concomitant priorities and have it accepted in large part because of the expertise that resides on campus.

In addition, the third mission of service creates principal-agent relationships between faculty and a wide range of players in the community, including nonprofit groups, economic development authorities, labor unions, and private businesses. In most cases, the faculty member is applying his expert knowledge to economic or policy problems in the region, sometimes as a consultant to local authorities, sometimes as a contributor to a task force producing a report or other tangible product. In many cases, both inputs and outputs are difficult to measure, especially when the satisfaction of principals in the community is hard to determine by colleagues on campus. Proxy measures are likely to prevail here as in other functions of the university, with service often defined as the simple fact of engaging in some kind of contribution to the university or the larger community.

The university is not the only entity in modern society with multiple and sometimes conflicting principals. The same phenomenon occurs in public bureaucracies:

> Multiple-principal arrangements are not unusual in organizations, since subordinate units often take orders from more than one superior unit (accounting, personnel); but an effort is ordinarily made by organizational leaders to impose order and consistency. In democratic politics, however, party competition tends to promote multiple-principal arrangements that are competitive rather than cooperative, as none of the parties wants the others to have unfettered control over the bureaucracy. And in a separation of powers system, competitive multiple-principal arrangements are actually built into the system by design. The president struggles with Congress over control of the bureaucracy, and, within Congress, House committees struggle with Senate committees. This is the way administrative accountability is supposed to work in a separation of powers system: it is literally true that no one is in charge.[6]

Just as the separation of powers creates internal struggles in government, so the presence of potentially competing principals within and outside the university means that authority is ambiguous. The agent with multiple principals is not under the complete control of anyone. No wonder, then, that education has been described as a loosely coupled system[7] and an organized anarchy.[8]

This situation provides both opportunities and uncertainties for faculty agents. The professor expected to address all three goals of the university—teaching, research, and service—sometimes lacks a clear sense of how time and effort are to be allocated among these objectives and thus how influence and authority are to be divided among competing principals. At the same time, this ambiguity allows agents to play one principal off against another and, in the process, to further their own self-interest. For example, a research grant with its schedule of tasks and its requirements of accountability can free the scholar from the demands of his department chair and his disciplinary colleagues; with enough outside support the researcher can buy out his teaching obligations or avoid requests for committee service. Yet his long-term commitments to the university keep him from being completely at the service of the program officer at the NSF or NIH.

The dilemmas and opportunities of the researcher facing multiple principals parallel the role of the university, or even higher education as a whole, in responding to the multiple expectations of the federal government. Colleges and universities increasingly serve as means for achieving such national priorities as advancing social equity, discovering cures for diseases, strengthening national defense, and improving agricultural productivity. Literally hundreds of categorical programs in dozens of federal agencies support research, student financial assistance, and education and training of many kinds; these federal programs, often bearing little relationship to one another, have harnessed colleges and universities in the service of larger national objectives.

Federal programs and agencies are structured around these objectives rather than consideration of the university as the mechanism for achieving these goals. Thus, on a single campus one can find members of the university community participating in the war on cancer, running an Upward Bound program for disadvantaged high-school students, or directing a grant from the National Endowment for the Humanities to develop a Renaissance studies curriculum. The university responds to many federal initiatives, each targeted to a different goal, each in isolation from the others; the university is the means for achieving many public ends.

The institution can turn these many opportunities to advantage if it chooses those federal activities that enhance its own priorities and goals. In the past, savvy players of the federal grants game have used federal funds to achieve university objectives while articulating these objectives in rhetoric that speaks of the national interest. But deans and provosts know that they do not control individual faculty, especially at research universities, where professors have substantial autonomy; these scholars enter into principal-agent relationships with science bureaucrats and other external players with little discussion or approval at the campus level. Thus, within the institution, individual faculty and administrators have responsibilities to different federal agencies pursuing various national goals. These external principals coexist with one another and with internal demands in an often uneasy manner that can increase ambiguity for on-campus agents.

The Common Interests of Principals and Agents

Principal-agent theory was developed in economics to explain conflict of interest and losses associated with asymmetric information in hierarchical organizations; it describes the ways in which principals seek to restrain or retrain the self-interest of their agents in order to maximize net profits. Yet colleges and universities are often marked by infrequent monitoring, minimal hierarchy, and substantial commonality of interests. What does this apparent divergence between theory and reality tell us about higher education?

One of the hallmarks of the university is the autonomy afforded its members. Deans and department chairs usually do not tell faculty members what to teach or how to set priorities in their research; full professors do not supervise associate and assistant professors the way a corporate vice president oversees her division heads. Even the most junior faculty member can often devise his own syllabus, choose his own topics for inquiry, and speak and vote at departmental meetings. Faculty are asked to do "very little that they don't choose to do. They get paid for reading, thinking, talking and writing about those things they find interesting and rewarding."[9]

Research grants enhance the autonomy given to individual faculty because they provide power over funds not controlled by the administration. "When I have a grant, I never have to ask the department for anything," said one scholar. "I bought this computer equipment with my grant, for example. I have more freedom with a grant. Then when the grant ends, I'm broke."[10] A researcher in another field corroborated this point by saying, "If you have money, you can do anything you want at [this university]." Faculty can also increase their salaries through grantsmanship; many are quite conscious of differences in compensation and expectations between professors in grant-rich departments, where three summer months at full pay may be the norm, and their colleagues in departments in which university funds are the sole source of income. While the administrator as principal is limited in her ability to reward her most productive agents, she can make it easier, through the provision of support and encouragement for sponsored research, for them to earn their own rewards. The official salary scale is less skewed, thus giving less offense to the egalitarian tradition in higher education. And, as principal, the administrator is promoting a system that produces the greatest tangible and intangible returns to the most productive faculty.

Even when the faculty member does not have research grants, however, he has substantial autonomy within the university. The academic community relies most frequently on peer pressure and moral suasion rather than monitoring and incentives to encourage desired behavior; the exception is the careful assessment process associated with the tenure decision. Thus, the university's measurement technique most often is a negative one—the absence of complaints. The assumption is that the faculty member will behave according to academic norms. As one professor explained the standards for teaching in his institution, "Being a good teacher means you're not so bad that students refuse to sign up for your classes . . . or complain to the chairman." This measurement technique is comparable to what Weingast and Moran call the "fire alarm" in Congress[11] or the thermostat metaphor that Birnbaum develops in Chapter 2 of this volume. Rather than exercise detailed oversight and control over the bureaucracy, members of Congress or academic administrators use constituent complaints to determine where problems exist, assuming that all is well in programs about which they hear nothing.

The fire alarm approach is well suited to the research university; the dean as principal has few incentives or sanctions available to change the behavior of tenured professors and no personal reward to engage in serious monitoring of faculty. Rather, she assumes that her faculty agents are effective in teaching, research, and service unless she hears otherwise, reserving her monitoring efforts for rare instances of gross malfeasance.

Ironically, the tenure system, which can cause so much conflict at the time of the individual decision, can reduce in the long run the need for extensive monitoring of agents by their academic principals. In the tenure process, colleagues and subsequently administrators review the candidate's teaching, research, and service, using a combination of actual and proxy measures of desired performance; the seriousness of the scrutiny matches the long-term implications of the decision for both the individual and the institution. During the probationary period, members of the university community gain accurate information on the performance of junior faculty and the goodness of fit between the candidate and the institution; those professors who successfully pass through the tenure process usually share the expectations and standards of their colleagues, thus reducing information asymmetries that demand monitoring. With job security guaranteed by tenure, many faculty develop a vested interest in their institutions and find their own futures linked to the success of their departments and universities. Perhaps most importantly, faculty and administrators believe deeply in the same set of academic values—academic freedom, rational inquiry, intellectual honesty, the importance of education, the challenges of the life of the mind.

These common values help to explain the relative absence of an important characteristic of the principal-agent relationship—conflict of interest. In a business, the entrepreneur has title to the residual of the enterprise; every dollar paid as wages or incentives to workers reduces her profits. In higher education, the profit motive does not exist, so the personal incentive of the principal and conflict with the agent recede. And, in the research university at least, principals and agents share many important goals so that conflict is muted.

Scholars from several different disciplines emphasize prestige as an important motivating force in higher education.[12] As Gross and Grambsch describe it,

> Prestige is a vague quality which accrues to organizations in a variety of ways. It conveys ideas of leadership, of power, and, above all, of excellence. . . . It is eagerly sought after by those who do not have it, and those universities that have achieved prestige do everything they can to uphold it. Prestige in universities is possibly of more significance than it is in other organizations. Attracting faculty and students, as well as foundation and other research grants, becomes considerably easier if the university is perceived to be a place of prestige.[13]

Prestige can derive from many factors, but national reputation is often based on high-quality doctoral programs, which demand research faculty. As noted above, success in prestige achievement makes it easier to obtain further outside grants, which in turn enhance prestige further.

But colleges and universities cannot buy prestige directly, for it is derived from the reputations of individual faculty members and of their aggregation into departments. Thus, faculty serve as agents for deans, presidents, and trustees who seek to improve institutional stature. Prestige is clearly related to intellectual excellence, but more accurately it is the perception of quality rather than an actual measure of quality; the ranking of departments and institutions on reputational surveys demonstrates the power of perceptions of quality. The way in which faculty strengthen those perceptions of the caliber of their thinking is through publication, which allows peers to form judgments of their work. Both faculty and administrators are quite clear about the role of research grants, from the federal government or other sources, in enhancing prestige. A successful grant-getter reported his status with these words, "Faculty who get grants are looked upon differently by the administration. . . . Dollars should not equate with prestige, but that seems to happen." From a political scientist: "In a meeting of social science department chairs, we were put down and told, 'You can't raise money.' We are definitely lower status in the minds of the senior administration." And even in fields such as English, grants matter: "The presence of outside money has real effects in the university. . . . Reviews don't say much in a fractious field like mine. But getting a grant means that you are hustling, you have contacts, you are refereeing. When there are so few grants in the humanities, it means something."

The approval of colleagues implicit in a successful grant proposal or an article in a refereed journal minimizes the dilemma of the principal who wants to measure the productivity of her agents; the dean or department chair can use grants and articles as indicators of quality, especially when the principal's own area of expertise is far removed from that of the faculty member she is evaluating. But, as noted earlier, when actual productivity is difficult or impossible to measure, proxy measures often prevail. In the dean-professor relationship, the proxy sometimes becomes the actual goal, as faculty are rated on the dollar value of the grants they receive or the number of pages published rather than their actual contribution to the store of knowledge. In such circumstances, the incentives provided by the principal to add to institutional prestige can have a perverse effect by enticing untenured faculty in particular to emphasize quantity over the quality of their scholarly output; the advancement of knowledge can be set aside as faculty repackage the same ideas for publication in several journals in an effort to meet institutional expectations or tenure standards.

Whether perverted or properly focused, the goal of academic prestige is widely shared among principals and agents; the grants and publications that help a university gain stature also advance the careers of individual scholars. The context in which professors seek to build prestige is the invisible college of colleagues in the same discipline around the world. The tangible products of scholarship that are most easily and objectively measured by principals both inside and outside the university are those that contribute to the goals of faculty members, campus administrators, and science bureaucrats alike.

Coupled Dependency

A traditional firm has a hierarchical structure in which each person is agent to a superior and simultaneously a principal to her subordinates; the vice president for marketing, for example, serves the chief executive officer of the corporation while supervising the work of division heads who report to her. Authority flows one way down the hierarchy. The classic government bureau is similarly hierarchical. The head of the National Science Foundation looks to the President and Congress for policy and budget decisions, while overseeing the directors of units responsible for biological sciences, antarctic research, science education, and so on. These administrators likewise supervise their bureaucratic subordinates, who are then principals to faculty researcher-agents.

Universities are less hierarchical, however, than either businesses or public bureaucracies. Described by one sociologist as "bottom heavy,"[14] institutions of higher education, especially research universities, have substantial power vested in departments and in individual professors, with few levels of structure above them. The autonomy of individual faculty that is a distinguishing characteristic of higher education leads to a special variation of agency that can be called "coupled dependency."

In the traditional principal-agent relationship, one party is always the principal and the other the agent in the contract. Doctor-patient, lawyer-client, employee-employer; in each case, the agent agrees to serve the principal's objectives rather than his own self-interest in return for some form of compensation. In higher education, the authority relationship can flow both ways *at the same time*. Each player is both principal and agent for the other. Rather than a hierarchical chain of control with a one-way flow of authority, the university might be described as a complex and sometimes messy system of coupled dependencies in which the direction of authority and control cannot be determined a priori.

Take first the relationship between faculty member and dean. The researcher seeks intellectual satisfaction, reputation in his discipline, greater autonomy, and promotion in his department; scholarly research and published results are important means for attaining these goals. The institution's objectives of higher status and greater prestige are derived by aggregating the successes of individual faculty; the institution cannot enhance prestige directly. Only through success in achieving his personal objectives can the faculty member be a successful agent for achieving the university's goals of increased income or reputation.

In a funny way, then, the relationship between administrator and faculty reverses. Certainly one important role for administrators is to facilitate the work of faculty by handling paperwork, allocating internal resources for proposal requirements, and providing infrastructure for the research enterprise. In most cases, the academic administrator comes from faculty ranks and shares faculty norms. In the role of supporter of faculty research, the dean or department chair can be seen as the agent facilitating the achievement of faculty goals. She can provide institutional support for laboratory facilities and can develop policies that encourage prestige-generating research; she expends university resources to further the research of individual professors. Such action, however, is not sufficient to achieve university goals of greater prestige. Only faculty themselves can produce the scholarly output that leads to the desired institutional objectives.

One need not look very far on campus to find other examples of coupled dependency between faculty and administrators. For example, at many institutions the provost has the power to appoint department chairs but finds it prudent to consult with leading faculty in the department in question before making a decision. Thus, the agents to be regulated are advising their principal on the way in which authority is to be exercised. The same phenomenon appears in other areas, such as decisions to offer a new academic program, to recommend a colleague for tenure, or to appoint a political theorist rather than a sinologist for an approved faculty line. Administrators look more like legitimators of decisions made by faculty than like principals monitoring unruly agents who require incentives and sanction to act in desired ways. Authority is a two-way relationship at many colleges and universities.

One reason for the difference between higher education and other organizations in modern society is that, in universities, knowledge is the end as well as the means.

> If consumer demands, job placements, and the interests of patrons were the only imperatives, academic organization would more nearly resemble standard bureaucratic organization. It is the primacy of cognitive materials and their internal shaping influence that make the difference, turning so many universities and colleges into knowledge-driven organizations driven by a bottom-up bias. Viability does not depend on the capacity of top-down commands to integrate parts into an organizational whole. Instead, it depends on the quality of the performance of the basic units as nearly self-sufficient entities that do the work of disciplines and reflect their concerns.[15]

Coupled dependency reflects the primacy of knowledge and the authority of those who expand and transmit it; knowledge-driven organizations depend for their success on the people intimately and directly involved with ideas.

External grants strengthen coupled dependency. Because research grants go to individuals rather than to institutions, they put more power in the hands of faculty entrepreneurs, who influence the long-term success of the institution as a whole. As specialized knowledge and the research model increasingly become the marks of high status, and as outside funds increasingly are essential for doing research, it is logical to speak of administrators as agents as well as principals in relation to faculty. Unless an institution is one of the few that is growing in size, administrators are forced by the reality of a steady-state faculty to seek prestige enhancements with the professors already on the roster. The limited pool of potential agents available to achieve institutional goals creates a small numbers problem in which those faculty with the specialized knowledge and intellectual ability to obtain research grants become more powerful as they bring prestige to the institution.

Administrators do have more control over a secondary source of prestige, the quality of students admitted to the institution. A prestige-maximizing model of the university uses the academic quality of undergraduates and the number of students enrolled as independent variables influencing the utility of the institution.[16] Since admissions policies for undergraduates are set centrally, administrators have more control than faculty over student characteristics, at least at the undergraduate level, as an influence on prestige improvement. But quantity and quality of students are significant in the prestige-maximization model because they improve conditions for faculty. More students mean higher tuition revenues and larger faculty size, and higher-quality students mean more stimulating classrooms; both factors produce better working conditions for faculty and allow institutions to attract better new professors, thus enhancing institutional prestige. The real locus of prestige improvement continues to be at the level of the individual professor.

The dramatic growth in federal support since World War II has reinforced existing patterns of increased autonomy and authority of faculty in comparison with the administrative principals on campus. It is no wonder, then, that Jencks and Riesman describe the actions of university administrators this way:

> The top management, while nominally acting in the interests of the board [of trustees], actually represents the interests of "middle management: (i.e., the faculty), both to the board and to the world. . . . Most university presidents see their primary responsibility as "making the world safe for academicians," however much the academicians themselves resent the necessary (and unnecessary) compromises made in their behalf.[17]

The relationship between faculty and administrators within the university is one of coupled dependency; both parties desire scholarly output for the prestige it brings to individuals and institutions alike. Since prestige is derived in large part from faculty actions and not from administrative efforts, power flows to those faculty who possess specialized knowledge and exercise the ability to garner outside grants and the prestige derived from them.

In a similar fashion, the relationship between researcher and science bureaucrat can also be characterized as coupled dependency. One significant factor is their common intellectual and professional background. Many administrators in the NSF and NIH come from campuses to the federal government, either as permanent employees or in temporary "rotator" positions. More importantly, academics serving on advisory committees and peer review panels make important funding decisions for these agencies; bureaucrats do not set priorities in isolation. Leading scientists from the National Academy of Sciences or the National Research Council suggest the most fruitful lines of research to be pursued in chemistry, mathematics, and other fields; the peer review process uses faculty scholars to judge the relative merits of individual proposals in addressing these funding priorities. In this perspective, the program officer serves as agent to the collective goals of research faculty as expressed by disciplinary leaders; she looks outward to faculty colleagues on campuses for policy direction rather than upward to bureaucratic or political superiors. The program officer's agents are also her principals.

Both on campus and in government agencies, the reversal of control can be seen as the dominance of specialization on the part of the professor, especially when contrasted with the inevitable ambiguity that accompanies multiple goals and multiple principals. University administrators and government bureaucrats both rely on faculty as agents to achieve their organizational goals. But because success in faculty goals is essential to reach university and governmental goals, these principals find themselves serving the interests of individual scholars at the same time that they are striving for their own objectives. The roles of principal and agent go both ways as faculty are linked in relationships of coupled dependency with administrators and bureaucrats. An analysis of the university as a web of mutually dependent principals and agents rather than an orderly chain of responsibility helps to explain the lack of hierarchy and the convoluted nature of decision-making in academic institutions.

Implications for Academic Governance

Looking at institutions of higher education through the lens of principal-agent theory illuminates many of the realities of academic life. Collegiality and shared governance are not just hoary anachronisms but constructs that reflect the patterns of authority and control inherent in coupled dependency. When faculty members and administrators are principals and agents for one another, shared governance is an appropriate decision-making structure.

An analysis of agency relationships also explains many of the frustrations of academic life. When authority lines are not clear, decision-making is slow; when hierarchy is limited, there is no chain of command for clear implementation of policies determined at the top. No wonder that garbage can theory[18] has such appeal to organizational behavior students and practitioners alike. With multiple principals, literally no one is in charge.

The principal-agent approach also provides one explanation for the dearth of presidents who are academic leaders. As the range of problems facing institutions multiply, from slowdowns in federal funding to increased demands for accountability from several constituencies, the ability of a shared governance structure to handle all of them is strained. It is no surprise, then, that more presidents devote an increasing proportion of their time to nonacademic matters. Not only are these often the issues impinging upon the institution, but the mechanisms to address nonacademic matters more closely resemble the hierarchical structure of corporations or bureaucracies. The president can exercise authority, make decisions, and see results more directly as principal in the business side of the institution, where the right to participate in governance is not jealously guarded by faculty agents.

This analysis also raised two pieces of cautionary advice to the players linked in relationships of coupled dependency in the university. The first is the need to be sensitive to the pressures placed by external principals on the university and to be explicit about the conflict or congruence of interests presented by these outside forces. Bureaucrats and other principals providing incentives to individuals and institutions, or state governments and other entities imposing sanctions, can exert strong influence upon their agents within the university. Unless those agents are clear about their own goals and the ways in which external players can change those goals, it is easy to allow external principals to set large parts of the internal agenda of the university. Outside funds provide tremendous opportunities for the advancement of institutions in addressing their missions, but the multiplicity of principals and agents in most colleges and universities can also make institutional goals less clear.

The second cautionary note reflects the fragility of coupled dependence on which successful governance depends. Common interests and shared goals, not hierarchical authority, make higher education work as well as it does. But in times of economic constraints, collegiality dissipates as campuses are marked increasingly by turf battles and difficulty trade-offs, with obvious implications for governance. But as this chapter has demonstrated, higher education lacks many of the characteristics of principal-agent relationships that contribute to effectiveness in other types of organizations; such characteristics include clear measures of success that are linked to profitability, incentives for workers that can be exercised by principals, and a hierarchical structure that vests authority up the chain of command. Without common interests, how can principals and agents work successfully in a bottom-heavy enterprise marked by nonprofit status and the absence of monitoring?

As the title of Clark's 1987 study of faculty reminds us, the academic life is truly "small worlds, different worlds." Principals and agents in research universities, where science bureaucrats play a significant role, represent reality in only a small proportion of all institutions of higher education; as one moves down the status hierarchy, faculty autonomy decreases and administrative authority increases, collegiality declines and bureaucracy grows. Thus, questions of governance look quite different depending upon the piece of the academic world one investigates. But a fresh look at university life provided by a principal-agent analysis raises issues of significance, not only for research universities but for the strength of the academic enterprise nationwide.

NOTES

Note: The research and writing of this chapter occurred while the author was a guest scholar at the Brookings Institution. She thanks David Riesman, Burton Clark, and her many colleagues at Brookings for their comments and suggestions on earlier drafts of this chapter.

1. To avoid confusion, this chapter assumes that the principal is female and the agent is male in all examples.

2. For summaries of principal-agent theory, see J. Hirschleifer and John G. Riley, "The Analytics of Uncertainty and Information—An Expository Survey," *Journal of Economic Literature* 17 (1979): 1378–1421; Terry M. Moe, "The New Economics of Organization," *American Journal of Political Science* 24 (1984): 739–77; A. Michael Spence, "The Economics of Internal Organization: An Introduction," *Bell Journal of Economics* 6 (1975): 163–72; and John W. Pratt and Richard J. Zeckhauser, "Principals and Agents: An Overview," in Pratt and Zeckhauser, eds., *Principals and Agents: The Structure of Business* (Boston: Harvard Business School Press, 1985), pp. 1–36.

3. Moe, 1984; Barbara J. Spencer, "Asymmetric Information and Excessive Budgets in Government Bureaucracies," *Journal of Economic Behavior and Organization* 3 (1982): 197–224; Barry Mitnick, "Agency Problems and Political Institutions," paper presented at the Midwest

Political Science Association, 1984; Jonathan Bendor, Serge Taylor, and Roland Van Gaalen, "Stacking the Deck: Bureaucratic Missions and Policy Design," *American Political Science Review* 81 (1984): 874–96; John E. Chubb, "The Political Economy of Federalism," *American Political Science Review* 79 (1985): 994–1015; Moe, "An Assessment of the Positive Theory of 'Congressional Dominance,' " *Legislative Studies Quarterly* 12 (1987): 475–520; B. Dan Wood, "Principals, Bureaucrats, and Responsiveness in Clear Air Enforcements," *American Political Science Review* 82 (1988): 214–34.

4. Armen A. Alchian and Harold Demsetz, "Production, Information Costs, and Economic Organization," *American Economic Review* 62 (1972): 777–795.

5. For further discussion of the implications of the input-output distinction, see Estelle James, "Decision-Making Structures and Incentives at American Higher Education Institutions," mimeographed, 1988.

6. Moe, "The New Economics of Organization," p. 768.

7. Karl E. Weick, "Educational Organizations as Loosely Coupled Systems," *Administrative Science Quarterly* 21 (1976): 1–9.

8. Michael D. Cohen and James G. March, *Leadership and Ambiguity: The American College President,* 2nd ed. (Boston: Harvard Business School Press, 1986).

9. Michael S. McPherson and Gordon C. Winston, "The Economics of Academic Tenure: A Relational Perspective," *Journal of Economic Behavior and Organization* 4 (1983): 172.

10. This and subsequent quotations from individual faculty members and administrators come from interviews conducted during the 1986–87 academic year at a number of colleges and universities.

11. Barry R. Weingast and Mark J. Moran, "Bureaucratic Discretion or Congressional Control? Regulatory Policymaking by the Federal Trade Commission," *Journal of Political Economy* 91: 1983.

12. For example, Jencks and Riesman as sociologists describe the professionalization of faculty, tracing the historical development of meritocratic values as a defining characteristic of academic life. Christopher Jencks and David Riesman, *The Academic Revolution,* 2nd ed. (Chicago: University of Chicago Press, 1977), ch. 1. Another sociologist, Martin Trow, analyzes the ways in which individual institutions seek comparative advantage in the market for factors of prestige such as distinguished professors, endowments, and scholarly honors; Martin A. Trow, "The Analysis of Status" in Burton R. Clark, ed., *Perspectives on Higher Education: Eight Disciplinary and Comparative Views* (Berkeley: University of California Press, 1984), pp. 132–164. Historian Roger Geiger traces the growth of disciplinary power and the development

of federal science policy as two factors influencing the research university. Roger L. Geiger, *To Advance Knowledge: The Growth of the American Research Universities in the Twentieth Century, 1900–1940* (New York: Oxford University Press, 1986). David Garvin presents an economic model of the university as a prestige-maximizing organization competing with other institutions in a market characterized by a number of highly segmented submarkets; David A. Garvin, *The Economics of University Behavior* (New York: Academic Press, 1980). Edward Gross and Paul Grambsch analyze changes in the organization and power structure of American universities between 1964 and 1971; obtaining and maintaining prestige is a leading goal of faculty and administrators in both years. Edward Gross and Paul V. Grambsch, *Changes in University Organization, 1964–1971* (New York: McGraw-Hill, 1974).

13. Gross and Granbsch, p. 100.

14. Burton R. Clark, "The Organizational Conception" in Clark, pp. 106–131.

15. Burton R. Clark, *The Academic Life: Small Worlds, Different Worlds* (Princeton: Princeton University Press, 1987), p. 268.

16. Garvin.

17. Jencks and Riesman, p. 17.

18. Cohen, March, and Olsen use the metaphor of the garbage can to explain the randomness of decision-making in higher education and other organizations; problems and solutions become attached to one another by accident or temporal proximity rather than rational linkages. Michael D. Cohen, James G. March, and John P. Olsen, "A Garbage Can Model of Organizational Choice," *Administrative Science Quarterly* 17 (1972): 1–25.

BIBLIOGRAPHY

Alchian, Armen A., and Harold Demsetz. "Production, Information Costs, and Economic Organization." *American Economic Review* 62 (1972): 777–95.

Allison, Graham. *Essence of Decision: Explaining the Cuban Missile Crisis.* Boston: Little, Brown, 1971.

Alpert, Daniel. "Performance and Paralysis: The Organizational Context of the American Research University." *Journal of Higher Education* 56 (1985): 241–81.

Arrow, Kenneth J. "The Economics of Agency" in John W. Pratt and Richard J. Zeckhauser, eds., *Principals and Agents: The Structure of Business.* Boston: Harvard Business School Press, 1985, pp. 37–51.

Bailey, Stephen K. "A Comparison of the University with a Government Bureau" in James A. Perkins, ed., *The University as an Organization*. New York: McGraw-Hill, 1973, pp. 121–36.

Bendor, Jonathan; Taylor, Serge; and Van Gaalen, Roland. "Stacking the Deck: Bureaucratic Missions and Policy Design," *American Political Science Review* 81 (1987): 873–96.

Besse, Ralph M. "A Comparison of the University with the Corporation" in James A. Perkins, ed., *The University as an Organization*. New York: McGraw-Hill, 1973, pp. 107–20.

Bok, Derek. *Higher Learning*. Cambridge: Harvard University Press, 1986.

Brown, William R. *Academic Politics*. University: University of Alabama Press, 1981.

Chubb, John E. "The Political Economy of Federalism." *American Political Science Review* 79 (1985): 994–1015.

Clark, Burton R. "The Organizational Conception" in Burton R. Clark, ed., *Perspectives on Higher Education: Eight Disciplinary and Comparative Views*. Berkeley: University of California Press, 1984, pp. 106–31.

Clark, Burton R. *The Academic Life: Small Worlds, Different Worlds*. A special report of the Carnegie Foundation for the Advancement of Teaching. Princeton: Princeton University Press, 1987.

Cohen, Michael D., and March, James G. *Leadership and Ambiguity: The American College President*, 2nd ed. Boston: Harvard Business School Press, 1986.

Cohen, Michael D.; March, James G.; and Olsen, Johan P. "A Garbage Can Model of Organizational Choice." *Administrative Science Quarterly* 17 (1972): 1–25.

Cyert, Richard M., and March, James G. *A Behavioral Theory of the Firm*. Englewood Cliffs, N.J.: Prentice-Hall, 1963.

Fama, Eugene F., and Jensen, Michael C. "Agency Problems and Residual Claims." *Journal of Law and Economics* 21 (1983): 327–49.

Fama, Eugene F., and Jensen, Michael C. "Separation of Ownership and Control." *Journal of Law and Economics* 21 (1983): 301–25.

Garvin, David A. *The Economics of University Behavior*. New York: Academic Press, 1980.

Geiger, Roger L. *To Advance Knowledge: The Growth of American Research Universities in the Twentieth Century, 1900–1940*. New York: Oxford University Press, 1986.

Gross, Edward, and Grambsch, Paul V. *Changes in University Organization, 1964–1971*. A report prepared for the Carnegie Commission on Higher Education. New York: McGraw-Hill, 1974.

Hirschleifer, J., and Riley, John G. "The Analytics of Uncertainty and Information—An Expository Survey." *Journal of Economic Literature* 17 (1979): 1378–1421.

Hirschman, Albert O. *Exit, Voice, and Loyalty: Responses to Decline in Firms, Organizations, and States.* Cambridge: Harvard University Press, 1970.

James, Estelle. "Cross-Subsidization in Higher Education: Does It Pervert Private Choice and Public Policy?" in Daniel C. Levy, ed., *Private Education: Studies in Choice and Public Policy.* New York: Oxford University Press, 1986, pp. 237–67.

Jencks, Christopher, and Riesman, David. *The Academic Revolution,* 2nd ed. Chicago: University of Chicago Press, 1977.

Jensen, Michael C., and Meckling, William H. "Theory of the Firm: Managerial Behavior, Agency Costs and Ownership Control." *Journal of Financial Economics* 3 (1976): 305–60.

Kogan, Maurice. "The Political View" in Burton R. Clark, ed., *Perspectives on Higher Education: Eight Disciplinary and Comparative Views.* Berkeley: University of California Press, 1984, pp. 56–78.

Lindblom, Charles E. *Politics and Markets: The World's Political-Economic Systems.* New York: Basic Books, 1977.

Lutz, Frank W. "Tightening Up Loose Coupling in Organizations of Higher Education." *Administrative Science Quarterly* 27 (1982): 653–69.

McPherson, Michael S., and Winston, Gordon C. "The Economics of Academic Tenure: A Relational Perspective." *Journal of Economic Behavior and Organization* 4 (1983): 163–84.

Mitnick, Barry, "Agency Problems and Political Institutions." Paper presented at the Midwest Political Science Association, 1984.

Moe, Terry M. "The New Economics of Organization." *American Journal of Political Science* 24 (1984): 739–77.

Moe, Terry M. "An Assessment of the Positive Theory of 'Congressional Dominance.'" *Legislative Studies Quarterly* 12 (1987): 475–520.

Niskanen, William A. *Bureaucracy and Representative Government.* Chicago: Aldine, Atherton, 1971.

Niskanen, William A. "Bureaucrats and Politicians." *Journal of Law and Economics* 18 (1975): 617–59.

Pfeffer, Jeffrey, and Salincek, Gerald R. *The External Control of Organizations: A Resource Dependence Perspective.* New York: Harper and Row, 1978.

Pratt, John W., and Zeckhauser, Richard J. "Principals and Agents: An Overview" in Pratt and Zeckhauser, eds., *Principals and Agents: The Structure of Business.* Boston: Harvard Business School Press, 1985, pp. 1–36.

Spence, A. Michael. "The Economics of Internal Organization: An Introduction." *Bell Journal of Economics* 6 (1975): 163–72.

Spencer, Barbara J. "Asymmetric Information and Excessive Budgets in Government Bureaucracies." *Journal of Economic Behavior and Organization* 3 (1982): 197–224.

Trow, Martin A. "The Analysis of Status" in Burton R. Clark, ed., *Perspectives on Higher Education: Eight Disciplinary and Comparative Views.* Berkeley: University of California Press, 1984, pp. 132–64.

Weick, Karl E. "Educational Organizations as Loosely Coupled Systems." *Administrative Science Quarterly* 21 (1976):1–19.

Weingast, Barry R., and Moran, Mark J. "Bureaucratic Discretion or Congressional Control? Regulatory Policymaking by the Federal Trade Commission." *Journal of Political Economy* 91 (1983): 765–800.

White, Harrison C. "Agency as Control" in John W. Pratt and Richard J. Zeckhauser, eds., *Principals and Agents: The Structure of Business.* Boston: Harvard Business School Press, 1985, pp. 187–212.

Williams, Gareth. "The Economic Approach" in Burton R. Clark, ed., *Perspectives on Higher Education: Eight Disciplinary and Comparative Views.* Berkeley: University of California Press, 1984, pp. 97–105.

Williamson, Oliver E. *Markets and Hierarchies: Analysis and Antitrust Implications, A Study in the Economics of Internal Organization.* New York: Free Press, 1975.

Wood, B. Dan. "Principals, Bureaucrats, and Responsiveness in Clean Air Enforcements." *American Political Science Review* 82 (1988): 213–34.

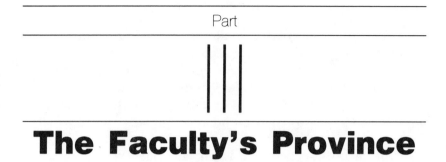

Part

III

The Faculty's Province

Although it is unarguable that faculties are essential to whatever calls itself a school, only in institutions of higher learning has that truism been made to justify—in widely varying degrees over time and place—faculty participation in the governance of the institution. That, as Walter Metzger reminded us in Chapter 1, is a tradition with deep historic roots; indeed it may be argued that, from Plato's Academy to Oxford's medieval beginnings as a corporation of scholars and masters, no real distinction between teacher and administrator existed. Scholars created their own schools, in which they taught and where they made and carried out the rules.

But separate classes of faculty and administrators have become well established in modern institutions of higher education for reasons that need no recounting here. If, in general, the two groups have learned to tolerate each other, their relationship remains typically wary and often today seems to be buffeted by new societal pressures, new actors on the scene, new role definitions, and still growing, if not novel, scarcities.

In Chapter 5, Jack H. Schuster examines how the faculty condition has been changing in recent years, thereby pointing toward the likely emerging problems for campus governance in the near future. His analysis of trends impinging upon the professoriate suggests that the faculty's role in governance has been challenged in a number of ways. Economic hard times, lack of mobility, internecine contention,

a deteriorating workplace, greater external constraints—
these are some of the interrelated factors that have characterized many American colleges and universities over the
1970s and 1980s. Schuster determines that they have taken
their toll on faculty morale. He also assesses their implications for shared governance and recommends corrective action.

In the face of such issues, Lynn H. Miller argues in
Chapter 6 that professors, as members of a profession, must
think clearly about their responsibilities to themselves and
to the community at large. Governance issues and areas of
faculty authority then can emerge more clearly. Miller suggests that when faculty members act in accordance with a
clear perception of their professional rights and duties, they
are more frequently the principals (in Kathryn Mohrman's
terminology) than they are merely agents in the institution's
authority structure. He also suggests, in keeping with arguments made by several other contributors to this volume,
that institutional prestige correlates strongly with true
professionalism on the part of the faculty.

In Chapter 7, Patricia R. Plante considers how critical it
is from her perspective as a university president to share
leadership with the faculty on a whole range of issues, and
not simply those of academic freedom and tenure, where
the faculty has traditionally had the central role to play.
Too much compartmentalization of governance functions,
she suggests, merely exacerbates "we-they" differences between faculty and academic administrators that cause needless friction within the institution. She urges fellow
administrators to behave in accordance with the precept
that collegiality should unite faculty with academic administrators in a common cause, and in a relationship where
equality of obligation, if not identity of function, is more
the rule than the exception.

5

Governance and the Changing Faculty Condition

Jack H. Schuster

The purpose of this chapter is to explore the link between the changing condition of the American faculty and the way in which campuses are governed. Two premises underlie the argument advanced herein. First, vigorous faculty participation in campus governance is highly desirable. This is taken as a given and is spelled out in other chapters of the book. Second, the extent and quality of faculty involvement in governance, as well as the outlook for future levels of participation, can best be understood by taking into account the general circumstances in which faculty members find themselves.

In order to comprehend better the hypothesized relationship between prevailing conditions and participation in governance, this chapter seeks (1) to present a brief historical overview of the faculty role in governance; (2) to describe relevant aspects of the current condition of the professoriate; (3) to suggest the implications of these conditions for faculty participation in the governance process; and (4) to proffer several recommendations that will bear upon the faculty's governance role. The focus throughout is on the *faculty* role in governance; this chapter does not purport to address directly the respective roles of other campus or off-campus constituencies.

The Evolution of the Faculty Role in Governance

The faculty's contemporary involvement in governance needs to be viewed within the context of recent academic history. The contention here is that the faculty's successes in achieving predominant influence over academic policy, at least at some kinds of institutions, have been partially offset during the post-1970 era, thereby undermining the faculty's influence in those areas that most matter to them.

The twentieth century has borne witness to remarkable growth in the faculty's influence over decisions that crucially shape academic policy. By all accounts, faculty members have come a long way since the turn of the century, when academic freedom was up for grabs, tenure with its protective shield was at a formative stage, and governing boards and presidents could, and often did, govern autocratically. Summarizing the historical progression, Clark Kerr has demarcated the "massive long-run developments in governance" into the following eras: dominance by governing boards began in 1636, giving way to presidential dominance after 1870, then to faculty dominance after 1920.[1]

Prior to the rise of American universities in the latter third of the nineteenth century, disregard for significant faculty involvement in campus decision-making was widespread.[2] The commonly held view relegated the faculty to a circumscribed role. This bias is reflected in a comment by Eliphalet Nott who, beginning in 1804, served as president of Union College for sixty-two years. Late in his extraordinary career President Nott was asked about the usefulness of faculty meetings. He replied, "I remember having one once, some thirty-six years ago, but I never wish to have another."[3] President Nott's reminiscence leaves aside how many contemporary presidents—or, for that matter, faculty members—would regard relief from faculty meetings over the next thirty-six years as a great blessing! Nott's comment nonetheless symbolizes the bad old days, when faculty prerogatives in governance were severely limited.

After the Civil War the faculty movement gained considerable momentum as the rapid expansion of knowledge spawned research and graduate faculties and began to transform faculty generalists into discipline-bounded specialists. Having survived eras of dominance by lay governing boards and autocratic president-ministers, the struggle for sufficient academic freedom to teach without excessive ideological restriction accelerated around the turn of the twentieth century. By the time the American Association of University Professors (AAUP) was established in 1915, much progress had been made toward shared governance. The next year, as one indicator of the importance of governance, the AAUP established its Committee T on College and University Government; the committee's purpose was (and is) to help shape standards for, and to monitor, governance practices. Faculty influence progressed steadily in the next decades, and by the middle of the 1960s the faculty had achieved a far greater measure of control over academic policy.

However, the faculty's momentum in governance has been blunted since the end of the 1960s. In 1968 Christopher Jencks and David Riesman, in their highly regarded book *The Academic Revolution*, described the impressive advances achieved by the faculty in their ability to influence academic policy.[4] Though this book was published at a time of considerable student upheaval, the "revolution" that Jencks and Riesman chronicled had little to do with student activism. Rather, *The Academic Revolution* spoke to the gradual attainment of control—achieved much more through evolution than revolution—by faculty over the university's academic core.

Ironically, their book appeared at just about the time that faculty influence on campus began to wane in some important respects. That is to say, having seized strategic strongholds within the ivory tower, the faculty found its influence in some areas of decision-making had been diluted.

This apparent reversal has both external and internal sources. External developments, particularly the scarcity of resources, has tended to push budgetary decisions upward within the organization and often beyond campus boundaries. Other "extracampus" factors include the sharp rise of student consumerism in an era of declining numbers of traditional-age college-bound students[5] and the propensity of accountability-minded, assessment-oriented agencies, external to the campus, to press their agendas upon the campus. As noted by the Carnegie Commission on Higher Education in 1973: "The greatest shift of power in recent years has taken place not inside the campus, but in the transfer of authority from campus to outside agencies."[6] Meanwhile, commensurate with those extracampus stimuli, campus and systems administrators quickly adapted to a more assertive management style—"management" was hardly a tolerable term within campus boundaries in 1970—in order to prompt adjustments to changing campus realities. In short, a "wide range of forces" was converging "to eclipse faculty autonomy."[7]

Viewed in the light of these powerful developments, the extent of faculty influence in governance perhaps reached its highest level circa 1968–70, and faculty members have been struggling ever since to preserve hard-won prerogatives. These developments demonstrate a preemption of faculty influence by other decision-makers. But just how much faculty influence has been diluted in various areas and in different kinds of campus settings is difficult to gauge, for, as argued later, relevant evidence about actual levels of faculty involvement in governance is hard to come by.

The Condition of the Professoriate

While too little may be known about the faculty's overall participation in the governance process, evidence abounds about the general condition in which faculty members find themselves. Basically the condition of the faculty is, perhaps as always, in flux, and further substantial changes may lie just around the corner. I will argue that these recent and anticipated shifts in the faculty condition will continue to pose formidable challenges for all who are committed to enhancing the faculty role in campus governance arrangements. Several aspects of the faculty's current status, considered together, establish a context for viewing the faculty's predispositions toward governance. Here are a half dozen salient factors:

First is compensation, one of the few elements of the faculty condition that can be reasonably well measured. The essential change is this: faculty members at American colleges and universities have lost approximately 10 percent of their earning power since 1970–71. Since that time faculty members have been the biggest losers among major nonagricultural occupation groups. While faculty salaries have rebounded modestly since 1981–82 (averaging an 1.9 percent annual increase in real terms), thereby wiping out approximately half of the previous losses, the net loss in real income since 1970 remains substantial.[8] (U.S. Department of Education figures show losses across all ranks in real faculty salaries between 1971–72 and 1985–86 of approximately 13 percent.[9]) It is difficult to forecast trends in compensation, but the undervaluing of the faculty's services relative to other professions must be counted as an area of continuing anxiety for American faculty members.

Second is the declining quality of the academic workplace. This indicator can be measured roughly. A number of surveys and studies (for example, Austin and Gamson 1983) demonstrate that the quality of the academic workplace has been steadily deteriorating, both in fact and—perhaps easier to document—in the faculty's perception of their environment.[10] To skim the surface, there has been a decline in clerical and secretarial support for faculty members; instrumentation for research lags badly; library budgets (adjusted for inflation) are down; office space is often very crowded; travel budgets are often ludicrous; deferred maintenance for campuses is mounting into the billions of dollars; and the proportion of poorly prepared students with whom faculty members must work is increasing. The confluence of these developments undermines morale and, presumably, the will to tackle tough campus problems.

A third aspect of the faculty condition reflects changing characteristics of the faculty members themselves. Two opposing demographic thrusts are evident. The first trend, well under way, might be referred to as the "congealing" of the faculty. The faculty is growing old, not just older. It is estimated that the modal age range of tenured faculty members will rise to 56–65 by the year 2000.[11] A further indicator is that today's faculty is already overwhelmingly tenured. In 1985 approximately 66 percent of all tenure-track faculty members enjoyed tenure, and the faculty is clustered increasingly in the top academic rank of full professor.[12] This trend in faculty characteristics suggests that a kind of hardening of the academic arteries has been occurring.

A countervailing thrust, however, is just beginning to surface. This development is predicated on a rapid turnaround in labor market conditions that will necessitate a great deal of hiring essentially between the present time and the year 2010.[13] Howard Bowen and I project the need to appoint roughly between 450,000 and 500,000 new faculty members during that period.

Aside from the tremendous challenge of recruiting such awesome numbers of well-qualified neophytes, this emerging development gives rise to what might be called a "bimodal faculty"—a faculty growing simultaneously older and younger. The faculty is aging— the so-called graying of the professoriate to which I have just referred—as the cohort of senior faculty members grows older and proportionately larger. Yet, at the same time as those older faculty members begin in the next several years to retire in large numbers, a burgeoning cohort of youthful faculty members will be hired to replace them. One consequence will be the shrinking number of faculty members in the 40-to-55 age range, often assumed to be at the height of their powers, experienced in the ways of the academy, and vigorous participants in campus affairs.

A fourth aspect of the condition of the American faculty has to do with stagnation and incongruence in the current academic labor market. Consider four of its characteristics. One, there has not been much new hiring in a long time, especially in the humanities and social studies. Two, there is in consequence relatively little mobility between campuses for faculty members. Three, campuses are relying increasingly on part-time faculty members. Four, a significant proportion of recent academic appointments appears to have resulted in a mismatch between faculty members' interests and the institutions' traditional priorities. Put another way, a kind of built-in incongruence has emerged between, on the one hand, the preferences of faculty members trained at research universities and acculturated in the modes of research and, on the other hand, the teaching-oriented values held by those campuses where many of them are employed. Many faculty members hired in recent years find themselves at campuses historically committed to effective teaching, where the research proclivities these new faculty members commonly bring with them are not highly prized. Dissonance results; morale suffers.

A fifth condition of the professoriate relevant for present purposes is the shifting reward structure for faculty. This trend is in some respects the converse situation of the mismatch just described. The shifting reward structure is a function in part of the strong buyers' market that has prevailed over the past decade and longer. Given an opportunity to hire bright newcomers with strong research orientations, some of those campuses—especially those heretofore committed primarily to effective teaching—have begun to change the reward structure for promotion and tenure. The long-standing status hierarchy of institutions, with research universities perched on the highest rung, shows no signs of weakening. Newly appointed faculty members, as noted, often appear to prize research and scholarship more than teaching, and many institutions, in turn, strive to emulate the research university model. In sum, faculty members are being called upon to be more productive in their research. This shift in campus expectations pressures nontenured faculty members, and it often frustrates faculty veterans on campuses with no strong tradition of research and scholarship as they watch the "rules of game" change on them. The result again is dissonance.

A sixth and concluding point concerning the faculty condition is uneven faculty morale. This situation is the product of many factors, among them the shifting reward system, the tight academic labor market, and decreased real earnings. Confusion results also from an array of crosscutting role expectations to which faculty members are currently subjected. They are being asked concurrently to reform the curriculum by making it more coherent, to reemphasize the importance of effective teaching, to increase research productivity, and to link their teaching and research more closely to the needs of business and industry. Still further, the faculty is being asked to accommodate expanded access to their institutions and to work more effectively with academically underprepared students. But at the same time, the faculty is routinely rebuked for having lowered academic standards and, accordingly, is being prodded to be more rigorous. All of these expectations, flying at faculty members from different directions, pose formidable challenges.

Unattractive pay, a deteriorating workplace, a congealing faculty, an inhospitable labor market, a stress-inducing reward system, and multiple role expectations—all these changes buffet the faculty. They tend to breed frustration and confusion, and to prompt disengagement on the faculty's part.

This is not to argue that the situation is universally terrible. In a few places it is, but on the whole the faculty condition is not awful. There are, to be sure, pockets of high faculty morale here and there; the "haves" appear to be in fine spirits.[14] And, indeed, few faculty members have opted to trade in academic careers for other pursuits.

But the toll of nearly two decades of erosion cannot be dismissed. The net result has been a faculty that is often demoralized, often dispirited. That is one of the central findings in *American Professors*.[15] And that conclusion is supported by the 1984 survey of five thousand faculty members conducted by the Carnegie Foundation for the Advancement of Teaching.[16]

Consequences for Campus Governance

What are the implications for campus governance of the half-dozen changes depicted above? What is the relationship between these changes in the faculty condition—or, put more subjectively, the faculty's *perception* of the changing quality of academic life—and campus governance arrangements? Indeed, a more fundamental query underpins that question: can *any* relationship be demonstrated between either the "objective" faculty condition or the faculty's perception of its own circumstances and the extent to which faculty members participate in the processes by which colleges and universities are governed? While it is not easy to substantiate a relationship between faculty participation in governance and the faculty condition, some speculations may be in order. To begin with, consider two conflicting hypotheses about the importance of governance to faculty members. Is shared governance so centrally important to faculty members that their devotion to it barely wavers whether the campus environment is upbeat or demoralizing? Or is the faculty's dedication to governance much more fickle, tending to slacken, rather than to intensify, in the face of adversity?

The first hypothesis holds that governance is crucially important to the faculty and, in the faculty's view, is a sine qua non of a healthy professional environment. Whatever the faculty condition, this view suggests that faculty influence over those matters that directly affect their professional destinies is unalterably a prominent part of the faculty agenda. Thus, whatever the status of the faculty may be at a given time, the impulse to achieve a larger share of control over academic life is deeply ingrained. For at least a core group of faculty leaders, the press for more influence is relentless, regardless of environmental conditions. The history of American higher education, as suggested previously, could be described in terms of a steady progression of the faculty's ability to influence, if not substantially control, academic policy, particularly academic personnel and curriculum decisions.

To be sure, the academic revolution/evolution referred to earlier was not universal. Pronounced differences among categories of institutions have been evident. The "mature" research universities were the primary site of the successful transformation. This movement, however, did not penetrate some other categories of institutions to such a marked degree, especially the burgeoning community colleges and the scores of normal schools that were metamorphosing into comprehensive state colleges. In all, though, the incremental changes over the decades added up to substantial faculty influence. And always, regardless of the setting, the faculty professed the importance of involvement and participation. To cite one example, although the forces giving rise to faculty unionism are complex, survey after survey has provided evidence that faculty members were moved to support unionism at least in part as a strategy for regaining control over their professional lives.

An opposing perspective is based on the observation that most faculty members in most settings do not choose to be involved in the governance process beyond the most rudimentary forms of departmental participation.[17] Viewed through that lens, despite the commitment of those few faculty activists on any campus who are deeply immersed in the process, governance remains a very peripheral concern to the rank and file. On almost any campus, faculty leaders—of senates and unions alike—are quick to point to the frustrations of trying to recruit colleagues for the essential work of governance. Faculty may rally when confronted by some "atrocity" they attribute to insensitive administrators or meddlesome outsiders, but deeper commitment to governance is unusual. In other words, ultimately most faculty members, when put to the test, appear to care little about governance—or at least so little that they decline to invest their own energies in the governance process beyond their immediate academic departments.

Thus, there are two streams of thought about the connection between the faculty condition and governance, and the connection at best is blurry. Reality appears to split the difference between these opposing tendencies. The faculty is often drawn more deeply into the vortex of campus governance by adversity, perhaps out of defensiveness, perhaps out of combativeness. At the same time, the faculty appears to be retreating from strong commitment to governance. Perhaps in part because of discouragement, the faculty can often be characterized by its indifference toward governance, and there is plenty of anecdotal evidence to establish that many faculty members have disengaged from what might be regarded as their historical responsibility to participate more meaningfully in the governance process. The result is ambivalence.

Part of the ambivalence about governance stems from the love-hate relationship between faculty and administration, which appears to continue undiminished. The more than five hundred interviews conducted for *American Professors* suggest a complex relationship. Faculty members often yearn for strong administrative strategic leadership, particularly in the establishment of goals and the creation of a vision for a campus. But a contrary phenomenon is the widespread, even pervasive, distrust and suspicion of administrative leadership.[18] It is a classic "Us versus Them" mind-set.[19] Another deterrent is surely the excessively complicated mechanisms that evolve, wherein checks and balances are so deeply embedded that change is hard to come by. (Of the twenty-nine campuses visited for the Carnegie Foundation's 1984 study of undergraduate education, Ernest Boyer has written: "Governance, on most campuses we visited, was an ineffective Rube Goldberg–like arrangement."[20]

Since the beginning of the 1970s faculty ambivalence about participation in shared governance may have spread. This ambivalence is seen in the "official" faculty rhetoric strongly endorsing the importance of faculty participation juxtaposed with faculty behavior—a common reluctance to invest the essential time necessary to become effectively involved. This suggests that faculty members must believe that their participation in governance is not so vital after all. Or it may demonstrate that all is well and that more extensive involvement in governance is not critically important.

Two more specific aspects of faculty participation in governance bear mention. The first of these is the apparent distancing of junior faculty members from the governance process. Here the faculty reward system figures prominently. The emphasis on scholarly productivity prior to tenure, along with the crosscutting roles and expectations for faculty members previously described, clearly leads to less involvement in the governance process for junior faculty members. They are being advised repeatedly by protective department chairs, among others, that their interests are best served by sticking close to the library stacks and to their laboratories and by ignoring as much as they can any of the campus "citizenship activities" to which they might otherwise fall prey.

Faculty involvement in the budgetary process is a second aspect. Richard Messinger, writing on the faculty role in budgetary decisions, raised the question "What are the joys and frustrations of active faculty participation in the budget process?" He answered succinctly: "Discussing the joys of participation is easy: there are none."[21] Significant faculty involvement in the budgetary process, where that is allowed, is very time-consuming. Accordingly, such commitment is hard to come by. Moreover, in an era of constrained resources, almost all major campus decisions—entailing shifts from one activity to another, or even net contractions—require inherently unpleasant choices. Significant involvement in such matters not only requires a great deal of time but can readily make enemies. And to repeat an earlier point, it is an investment of time that the faculty reward system ordinarily does not appreciate. That dilemma lies at the crux of the problem.

Recommendations

Several courses of action might be undertaken to enhance the quality of faculty participation in governance.

First, the faculty reward structure system needs to be modified to recognize the importance of committing time to the governance process. Henry Mason has observed that "Somehow, the rewards for participation in the governance of the institution must be perceived once more as significant; and the selection of the various faculty representatives must again result in choices which indeed constitute the most legitimate voice of the faculty."[22] Unless a reward system acknowledges the importance of university service, faculty members understandably will continue, on the whole, to be disinclined to participate meaningfully in that process.

There are various ways to recognize—and suitably reward—involvement. One such model can be found at Smith College in Northampton, Massachusetts. Smith's polity has provided for the academic personnel system to give equal weight to what might be called "campus citizenship"—right alongside teaching and scholarship. Thus, the "quality" of involvement in governance—service on key committees, for instance—is formally recognized as a criterion, on the same footing with the criteria of teaching and scholarship, for determining merit pay. This model acknowledges the importance of serious faculty participation in the affairs of the institution and ensures that participation counts far more than is ordinarily the case in reaching key personnel decisions (promotion, tenure, retention) and determining compensation. Leaving aside whether so bold a formula is necessary to induce quality faculty participation, my strong impression is that campus governance at Smith is very effective from both faculty and administrative perspectives, and that a generally high faculty esprit obtains there in part because the faculty is involved up to its collective ears in the governance of the campus. I suggest that this model can be adapted to many campus settings by moving beyond hollow rhetoric that praises the value of university service and too often ends there.

A second objective is based on the importance of preparing cohorts of future professors to take the governance role more seriously. This is predicated on the need for graduate schools and graduate divisions to pay much more attention to the preparation of those who will begin academic careers in the future. While generalizations are hazardous, graduate schools and graduate divisions as such currently have very little to do with the preparation of future professors. That process of preparation is largely decentralized to the control of academic departments and, in most respects, that is where the preparation ought to take place.

However, the traditional way of training would-be professors largely ignores two areas. One is the lack of emphasis on teaching skills for those teaching assistants who will become professors. (That area of neglect may well be changing for the better, but that is another topic.) The more relevant area of oversight, almost universally ignored in graduate training, has to do with the acculturation of future professors to the academic norms of our colleges and universities. There are ways that graduate schools and divisions can promote and facilitate on a campuswide basis efforts to help would-be academics to understand something of the history and the traditions and the values of academic life. Accordingly, conveying some of the rudiments of academic freedom, tenure, and shared governance to prospective faculty members would provide a healthier and more realistic introduction to the norms and principles of academic life. In fact, broad-gauged seminars for teaching assistants, structured along these lines, exist at some major universities (for instance, the University of California–Davis and Florida State University). Such efforts enable faculty members–to–be to move beyond the much more narrowly focused acquisition of expertise in their own discipline.[23]

A third area has to do with building an adequate data base about campus governance. The paucity of current empirical data about the practice of governance is striking. Logan Wilson has observed that "most of the extensive literature on academic governance, unfortunately, represents authors' opinions rather than any systematic inquiry into what the various participants perceive and prefer."[24] And that judgment, set forth in 1979, is no less true today.

Updating the status of campus governance is not easy to do because hard empirical data have been sparse over the past decade or more. By contrast, policy statements about governance abound: the Carnegie Commission on Higher Education, the Carnegie Foundation for the Advancement of Teaching, the American Association of University Professors, the American Council on Education, and the American Association for Higher Education are among the numerous groups that have proffered policy statements on campus governance.[25] In addition, a number of helpful case studies have been published, though many of those have focused on the role of external coordinating agencies or on the strategic-planning process.

Still other governance-related topics have received considerable attention. For example, much was written about the student role in governance, prompted by the student activism that was highly visible from, say, 1964 to 1971. As activism dissipated, that corpus of literature began to dry up. A deluge of writing about changes in governance attributable to the advent of collective bargaining appeared during the late 1960s through the mid-1970s. And much is being written these days about that important but amorphous topic, campus leadership.

In all, the recent literature on governance has been dominated by case-specific descriptions and by a lot of prescription. There is, however, little direct evidence to determine whether the norms of faculty participation in governance have, in fact, shifted since the end of the turbulent 1960s. Very little is known about the extent to which faculty members today participate in various kinds of decisions on what kinds of campuses. That was not always the case: an extensive campus-by-campus survey on governance was conducted during the winter of 1969–70 by Committee T of the American Association of University Professors.[26] This survey provided a baseline "measurement" of faculty involvement in decision-making. However, nothing of comparable ambition has been attempted since then. This means that the academic community has very little to go on in efforts to understand just how faculty members participate in campus governance and what shifts have occurred since around 1970.

I am encouraged by the establishment of the National Center for Postsecondary Governance and Finance at the University of Maryland–College Park. Generously funded by the U.S. Department of Education, the center has launched a variety of important projects dealing with campus governance and finance. I believe the center has an opportunity to develop baseline data about the conditions of campus governance. I would hope that in the next several years the center would help investigate the extent of faculty participation in governance in order to move beyond speculation and prescriptive rhetoric toward more precise understanding of the state of campus governance.

The faculty's involvement in campus governance is in flux. It is marked by ambivalence, often indifference, sometimes impressive commitment. Too little is understood systematically about what proportions of faculty members participate in what kinds of governance activities. It is reasonable, nonetheless, to assume that vigorous faculty involvement in governance will make for healthier campus environments. And conversely, one might suppose, improved campus conditions will attract larger proportions of faculty members to engage willingly in the hard day-to-day activities—beyond responding to the occasional crisis—that constitute effective campus governance.

NOTES

1. Clark Kerr, *The Uses of the University*, 3rd ed. (Cambridge: Harvard University Press, 1982), p. 180.

2. See W. H. Cowley, *Presidents, Professors, and Trustees: The Evolution of American Academic Government*, ed. Donald T. Williams, Jr. (San Francisco: Jossey-Bass, 1980).

3. T. Dwight, *Memories of Yale Life and Men* (New York: Dodd, Mead, 1963), p. 110, cited in W. H. Cowley, *Presidents, Professors, and Trustees*, pp. 80–81.

4. Christopher Jencks and David Riesman, *The Academic Revolution* (Garden City, N.Y.: Doubleday, 1968).

5. See, for example, David Riesman, *On Higher Education* (San Francisco: Jossey-Bass, 1980).

6. Kenneth P. Mortimer and T. R. McConnell, *Sharing Authority Effectively: Participation, Interaction and Discretion* (San Francisco: Jossey-Bass, 1978).

7. Carnegie Commission on Higher Education, *Governance of Higher Education: Six Priority Problems* (New York: McGraw-Hill, 1973), p. 1.

8. Hirschel Kasper, "Mastering the Academic Marketplace: The Annual Report on the Economic Status of the Profession, 1987–88," *Academe* 74, 2 (March–April 1988): 3–16.

9. Joyce D. Stern, ed., *The Condition of Education: Postsecondary Education* (Washington, D.C.: National Center for Education Statistics, U.S. Department of Education, 1988), vol. 2, Table 2:15–1, p. 104.

10. Ann E. Austin and Zelda F. Gamson, *Academic Workplace: New Demands, Heightened Tensions* (Washington: ASHE-ERIC Higher Education Research Report No. 10, 1983).

11. Ernest L. Boyer, *College: The Undergraduate Experience in America* (New York: Harper & Row, 1987).

12. U.S. Department of Education, *Digest of Education Statistics, 1987* (Washington, D.C.: U.S. Government Printing Office, 1987).

13. Howard R. Bowen and Jack H. Schuster, *American Professors: A National Resource Imperiled* (New York: Oxford University Press, 1986).

14. Bowen and Schuster, *American Professors*. See also Burton R. Clark, *The Academic Life: Small Worlds, Different Worlds* (Princeton, N.J.: Car-

negie Foundation for the Advancement of Teaching, 1987); R. Eugene Rice and Ann E. Austin, "High Faculty Morale: What Exemplary Colleges Do Right," *Change* (March–April 1988): 51–58.

15. Bowen and Schuster, *American Professor.*

16. Carnegie Foundation for the Advancement of Teaching, "The Faculty: Deeply Troubled," *Change,* 12,4 (Sept.–Oct. 1986): 31–34. See also Boyer, *College.*

17. Carnegie Foundation for the Advancement of Teaching, National Survey of Faculty, 1984, cited in Boyer, *College Professors,* Table 46, p. 243.

18. Jack H. Schuster, "Faculty Vitality: Observations from the Field," in Roger J. Baldwin, ed., *Incentives for Faculty Vitality* (San Francisco: Jossey-Bass, 1985).

19. Barbara J. Howell, "Four Issues in Contemporary Campus Governance: The Costs (And Benefits) of Faculty Participation," *Academe* 68, 1 (Jan.–Feb. 1982): 5A.

20. Boyer, *College Professors,* p. 242.

21. Richard J. Messinger, Jr., "Four Issues in Contemporary Campus Governance: The Woes (and Joys) of Faculty Participation in the Budget Process," *Academe* 68, 1 (Jan.–Feb. 1982): 6A.

22. Henry L. Mason, "Four Issues in Contemporary Campus Governance: The 1966 Statement Revisited," *Academe* 68, 1 (Jan.–Feb. 1982): 4A.

23. Jules B. Lapidus, "Preparing Faculty: Graduate Education's Role," *Bulletin,* 39, 9 and 10, American Association for Higher Education, May–June 1987: 3–6. Jack H. Schuster and Daniel W. Wheeler, *Enhancing Faculty Careers* (San Francisco: Jossey-Bass, in press).

24. Logan Wilson, *American Academics: Then and Now* (New York: Oxford University Press, 1979), p. 107.

25. For example: American Association of University Professors, Association of Governing Boards, and American Council on Education, "Joint Statement on Government of Colleges and Universities" (1966) in *AAUP Policy Documents and Reports* (Washington: AAUP, 1984 ed.), pp. 105–110.

26. Report of the Survey Subcommittee of Committee T, *AAUP Bulletin* 57 (Spring 1971): 68–124.

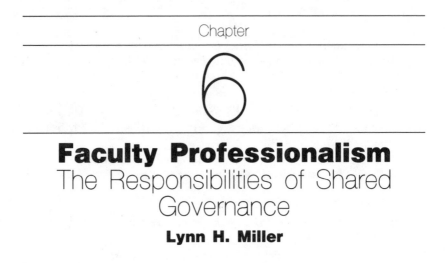

Chapter

6

Faculty Professionalism
The Responsibilities of Shared Governance
Lynn H. Miller

If there is a single leitmotif in current discussions of shared governance in American colleges and universities, it is that our traditional views and expectations must change in keeping with the
changing forces at work both on and in our educational institutions.
Externally, both the federal and state governments now impinge
on higher education in novel ways, while shifting demographics
have produced a competition for students and funding that requires
reordered priorities from academic administrators. Internally, the
academic hard times of the 1970s and 1980s sharply reduced the
demand for faculty members and, with that, the only real power
they had vis-à-vis their institutions. Faculty mobility, opportunities
for advancement or for career changes, all have been and generally
remain much restricted.

Meanwhile, in response to all these trends, colleges and universities have moved more and more toward corporate models of
governance, so that faculty members increasingly seem shut out of
a process in which many of them, or (they may suppose) their
predecessors, were once involved. Feeling themselves disenfranchised within their own institutions, they see their best hope for
the future in becoming "less sole-source dependent on universities,"
acting like diners who graze over the menus of several restaurants
rather than fill up at home, as they have done traditionally. If they
can satisfy themselves at this, they may, by the turn of the twenty-
first century, "look upon their universities as a base from which
to transact their more important business."[1]

Such a vision scarcely assumes an involvement in governance of the "home" institution; rather, it portrays faculties who will surely regard university service, even more than they do today, as a waste of time. For these reasons, we are assured that the presumed golden age in which we participated in important ways in governance, if that age ever did exist, cannot return, and that as a result, "the model of shared leadership must change; it can no longer reflect a nostalgic view of the mythical community of scholars."[2]

Too much nostalgia, it is true, may impinge upon one's grasp of reality. Yet, as a social scientist, I am respectful of the mythic power of collective beliefs; as a faculty member with some experience in the faculty senate of my own university, I am more than ever convinced that this view of ourselves as constituting a community of scholars has for centuries had too much to commend it to allow it to be casually discarded now. Indeed, that idea must be sustained as our central, empowering concept if the nation's institutions of higher learning are to continue to do the job they are meant to do, and if we as faculty members are to maintain the integrity of our profession.

The Faculty's Responsibilities

The word profession is the key. The central, almost the only, purpose behind faculty participation in the shared governance of academic institutions is to maintain and enhance the professionalism of higher education. Conversely, the only justification for the faculty's right to a share in governance, or for our other rights of academic freedom and tenure, lies in that same professionalism.[3]

Actually, those of us faculty members who have been deeply involved in shared governance find it more accurate to describe that activity as our professional *duty*, the obligation we owe ourselves and our colleagues to keep secure our *rights* of tenure and academic freedom. Only we who are professors and scholars can, by definition, maintain the standards and values of our profession and all that is connoted therein. If we fail at this task, we will have failed our profession, perhaps even destroyed it, for outside forces will then set the standards and make the rules for us.

So, the first task of faculty governance amounts to policing ourselves to maintain the standards of our profession. This much is surely obvious to any of us who have thought at all about these matters. This is the aspect of self-governance with which we are most familiar, entailing the important tasks of promotion and tenure reviews by faculty peers and—fortunately, less often—the kinds of investigations that may become necessary when individual faculty members are charged with conduct that violates some standard of the profession.

Well-run institutions of higher learning generally have procedures for this kind of maintenance of standards firmly in place. Where they do not exist, or are faulty, it is essential that the faculty create them, always by way of showing how this kind of faculty governance can help legitimize the authority of deans and presidents. Sensible administrators welcome such procedures for the simple reason that judicious peer review points the way to proper action and should lead the administrative officer to a decision that, even when it impacts drastically on the life of a faculty member, is virtually unassailable because it is the product of a prior professional judgment.

Of course, conflicts are sometimes inherent in this process, as when a peer review is overridden by a dean's or provost's decision in a case of tenure or promotion, but as a general rule, the more rigorous and professional the peer evaluation, the greater the likelihood that the administrative officer will concur and not dissent from whatever it advises. It is in this way that the faculty's "mere" power to advise may, and generally does, become nearly indistinguishable from the binding decisions that follow on behalf of the institution.

These familiar professional responsibilities are essentially related to faculty members' claims to a particular disciplinary expertise, at least in the usual initial round of peer reviews for tenure and promotion. Established physicists judge aspiring physicists, historians judge historians. But our professional responsibilities and our claims to a share in decision-making and governance do not end at the boundaries of our disciplines. That, too, is familiar to us when peer review for tenure and promotion extends, as it usually does, to college- or university-wide committees of faculty members from outside the discipline of the individual being considered. Most faculty members at most institutions of higher learning recognize, if sometimes grudgingly, that their professional obligations extend this far as well. They may not like giving their time to a college-wide committee on promotions, but they are at least likely to recognize its essentiality to the successful running of the institution.

What is frequently more difficult for many faculty members to see—and particularly so for those whose career rewards are most closely tied to a particular discipline—is that their obligations to the advancement of academic values and standards do not end there. As professional educators, faculty members have unique and central roles to play in shared governance that include but go far beyond departmental duties, whether or not they take on assignments through their faculty senates or collective-bargaining units. If they do not continue to fill those roles, there is no assurance that the place of higher education in the nation's life will be preserved and strengthened. Faculty participation in governance is vital to preserve the integrity of the academy and, in the final analysis, to enhance the life of the mind. It is the only way to maintain the academic profession in the large sense or even, probably, our professions in the narrower sense of separate intellectual disciplines.

Faculty Priorities Are Campus Priorities

Here is a short list of the kinds of things faculty members owe to their colleges and universities, as well as to their profession, none of which are the primary responsibility of others either within academic institutions or the world beyond. Together, they amount to a checklist for getting the institution's priorities straight.

1. *To insist upon the centrality of the educational mission.* In a world in which college presidents are increasingly fund-raisers and lobbyists, in which boards of trustees are dominated by captains of industry and technology, and in which grantsmanship is the major preoccupation of many administrators and faculty alike, it is easy to lose sight of this basic reason for our existence. No one but the faculty has the capacity to keep education at the heart of our institutional lives and to monitor its effectiveness. To do so requires vigilance and, frequently, concerted action beyond the departmental level. Even when we think our nonfaculty colleagues share this commitment with us, we may wonder what it really means to them. I recall hearing the chairman of the board of trustees of an important university, after he had been charged with ignoring his faculty's authority, concede merely that the "faculty is the critical component in delivering our educational message." Such an attitude

should remind us at least that the educational mission of the faculty is not confined to the students in our classrooms.

We faculty members have not always insisted upon the centrality of our commitment to education. Had we done so, there would have been no spate of recent scandals in the United States involving intercollegiate athletic programs and no skewing of priorities in many other universities where similar scandals may simply be waiting to happen. That we have not, collectively as faculty members, always insisted that our institutions get their priorities straight was made embarrassingly clear in Ernest Boyer's 1986 report for the Carnegie Foundation, which indicted our undergraduate colleges for their educational failures.[4] No doubt, many of us have felt too complacent with our own reward system and too powerless in the face of national trends to suppose we might correct the ills Boyer outlined. But if we are to maintain our integrity as professional educators, we must initiate reform within our home institutions, where necessary, and support it where it has been begun by others. To do less is to abdicate the first of our responsibilities.

2. *To enhance the relationship between scholarship and effective teaching.* None but those of us who practice it as a profession can appreciate fully the symbiotic intertwining of good teaching and scholarly inquiry outside the classroom. No doubt the layperson often assumes that our free summers, our less than forty hours each week—not infrequently, nine or even six—in front of a class, suggest a shirking of real labor. Perhaps such assumptions sometimes affect the minds even of academic administrators (who knew better when they themselves were faculty members) as they remain chained to desks long after we have left our classrooms and our students for the solitude of our studies and laboratories.

But we at least know that the "publish or perish" cliché has always slid over the essential point (apart from the sad fact that some hapless academics have done both) that scholarly investigation and inquiry, whether or not it leads to publication, is what justifies our claims to be educators. This understanding should have certain very practical imperatives for us collectively as members of faculties.

It means that we have an absolute obligation to ourselves, to our students, and to society at large for at least all of the following: (a) to invite the rigorous evaluation of our own effectiveness in the classroom; (b) to support every constructive effort that can be made institutionally to improve our own teaching effectiveness and that of our colleagues (including, especially, our colleagues-in-waiting, our graduate students); (c) to support sabbatical programs that promote scholarly inquiry as opposed to more time off; (d) to engage conscientiously in peer review for merit, not back-scratching; (e) to work not just for reduced teaching loads but for curricular innovations that will help stretch our minds and those of our students. These and comparable matters can be effectively addressed only through faculty participation in governance. The ablest academic administrators cannot make these things happen without widespread support from their faculty, whereas even weak administrators should find them irresistible where a united faculty initiates and strongly lobbies for them.

3. *To stimulate interdisciplinary connections.* Our disciplinary divisions, though they are organizationally convenient and basic to our sense of what it means to acquire expertise in a subject, can become intellectually stultifying to the extent that they seal us off from the larger universe of ideas. Evidence abounds that much of the most exciting research being done today is at the gray edges between established disciplines. Some would argue that the most important intellectual breakthroughs almost always occur at a disciplinary frontier, because it is those areas that our traditional cognitive maps have discouraged us from exploring.

When faculty members participate in their university senates, collegial assemblies, or bargaining units, they enter interdisciplinary forums, although no one would argue that the work of these bodies is typically interdisciplinary in any intellectually respectable sense of the term. Yet that work surely will include reminders of various curricular issues that cross departmental lines and of other professional commonalities. At its most rewarding, it may act serendipitously to bring together minds that will stimulate each other once the meeting has ended.

Whether the end result is an interdisciplinary research project or a new cross-disciplinary course or program, the instrumental effect played by the faculty governance structure is no less important to the health of the institution than the more direct policy outputs of faculty governance. In fact, the serendipitous results themselves become part of the institutional profile and, therefore, another mark that the faculty *is* engaged in governance in the broadest and most important sense of the term. I cannot imagine any way in which these crucial interdisciplinary stimuli can be brought about, and certainly no way in which they can then be harnessed to a productive purpose, without a deep commitment by faculty to participate in the life of their institution beyond the boundaries of their own disciplines.

4. *To support traditional disciplinary expertise and departmental integrity.* This is the converse of the previous item, not its contradiction, for it would be foolish to argue that our responsibility to involve ourselves in governance beyond the level of the department is somehow meant to denigrate the vital need for the members of each discipline to continue to police themselves. Service within the department is also an essential part of a faculty's self-governance.

In keeping with the department's primary responsibility for its own curricular and personnel matters, issues that involve overreliance on part-time instructors may be most effectively addressed here, since it is within the department that the damages of this practice may first be felt.[5] We also have a professional responsibility to attend to the appropriate training of our successors through careful supervision of student assistants, including attention to the ways in which they are used to assist in undergraduate instruction, providing them with effective training for the classroom, monitoring their teaching practice, and more. There may be legitimate differences of view on these matters, so much so that to leave policy issues in the hands of deans or departmental chairs may be dangerous or, at the least, demoralizing. For the faculty not to get involved in them is simply unprofessional.

Just as important is the support that only faculty can give to maintaining essential, if underenrolled, disciplines during their hard times. No doubt, more than one foreign language program has been spared the ax in recent years by the rallying cry of faculty members from other disciplines (my own university's tiny Classics Department probably was saved during a budget crunch by just this kind of outcry by faculty from many other disciplines). Other departments will be saved in the future if their colleagues behave in similarly responsible fashion when undergraduates again reorder their shopping lists for majors, as they are bound to do. All of these matters entail the governance of ourselves and our profession, and of the particular academy where we reside.

5. *To articulate the societal benefits of support for higher education.* Professional educators ought to be uniquely qualified to explain the myriad ways in which the acquisition of knowledge contributes to the quality of life. We would not be members of the teaching profession if we did not believe deeply in that connection. We see it verified every time our students sense some new power of the

intellect they have not imagined before. But we tend to be passive about asserting it to the wider community, either because we incorrectly suppose that this truth is a truism that needs no further demonstration to the public, or that this is a specialized branch of teaching that has been delegated to our chief administrative officers. After all, aren't college presidents paid to make just this case to legislators, corporate donors, and other taxpayers?

Yet, why should the community necessarily share our assumptions if their principal awareness of the academic institution in which we labor is confined to television and newspaper reports on the football season, the arrest of our students on drug charges, the appointment of a new business school dean, or the need for yet another tuition hike? How can a president who may have been, say, a geologist many decades ago make a persuasive case for the good that will flow to Wacko Corporation and the public generally if its officers agree to endow a chair in medieval French literature?

It is not that we professors can all become lobbyists, if we are in public institutions, or development officers, if our schools are private. But we should be ready to respond with the soundest arguments we can muster whenever it is appropriate to assist in a funding effort. College presidents may find it comparatively easy today to make the case for providing our students with literacy in computer languages; we may have the more difficult task of tackling the disgraceful problem of this nation's illiteracy in foreign languages. Provosts may help to secure generous support for research widely expected to have obvious beneficial applications to all our lives, such as superconductivity or a cure for the latest viral epidemic; we alone may have the knowledge and experience to persuade skeptical funding sources of the more indirect benefits of research in paleontology or number theory.

At a time when more lip service, at least, is being paid to the needs of education in the United States than has been the case for many years, professional educators have a clear responsibility to help bring about the right policy results. Among us there should be some who are creative enough to produce this century's equivalent to the Morrill Act of 1862, perhaps the most farsighted single contribution to higher education and the society at large that America has ever made. And there should be many others with the energy and conviction needed to counter the know-nothing opposition to public support for higher education that has recently worn the mask of public policy in this country. We betray our professional responsibilities and our society's future whenever we fail to join this battle.

6. *To anticipate changing societal needs and help shape higher education's response to them.* One of the presumed advantages of our expertise in various disciplines is an understanding of complex phenomena that should permit us to see where trends and patterns may be taking us before they are visible to the more casual and less-informed observer. Therefore, one of our most important obligations to society ought to be to assist in realistic planning for the future. Yet, too often we are so absorbed with protecting our traditional bits of disciplinary turf that we fail to act responsibly in this regard—as when we continued to turn out more and more teachers in spite of the post–baby boom decline in the birthrate; too often we are complacent in assuming that traditional curricula and academic modes for organizing the intellectual universe are meeting society's needs—as became apparent, frequently with an overreaction in the direction of "relevance" during the student (and faculty) upheavals in academe in the 1960s.

This is, of course, a particular piece of the argument about our responsibility to demonstrate the connections between education and the quality of life. It has been manifested in recent years in massive efforts by many elite colleges and universities to enroll far more students from previously underrepresented sectors of the population, in the refusal of a substantial number of scientists in academic institutions to work on Star Wars research, and in the codes of conduct developed first by scientific investigators for acceptable practice in the new possibilities for genetic engineering.

Such policies are not usually at the core of what we think of as involving faculty in the governance of academic institutions, but all of them were produced by bringing academic expertise to bear on societal problems and policies, problems which themselves were largely discovered first by academic analysis. It is difficult to think of any issues that can have more far-reaching consequences for society's future than these and others like them. It is impossible to imagine more important tasks for faculty governance of the profession than these.

One aspect of this professional obligation requires us to shake the very organizational tree of our own academic institutions where restructuring may better serve the community's educational needs of the future. It means even a willingness on the part of faculty to invent new disciplines where they are needed in response to emerging social and intellectual requirements of the times in which they find themselves.[6] That is to take charge of the direction of higher education in the most potent way possible and, again, in a way for which only those who are educators by profession should assume the authority.

The Centrality of the Faculty in Governance

This nonexhaustive list of our professional obligations as faculty members may seem so familiar as to be platitudinous. At the most general level, the assent of academics to these propositions is like that in support of motherhood: as vaguely shining ideals they neither provoke controversy nor drive real progress in our social institutions.

That, of course, is the problem, for these matters are central to our profession and central to the academy. Taking them seriously *should* induce action by us that may frequently provoke controversy but that will constitute the real engine of progress in higher education. To act upon them is to advance both our rights and the finest values of the academy. To act in accordance with these professional responsibilities is to share in the governance of our academic institutions.

Leaders in any faculty should also recognize that not all their colleagues can or should be expected to respond identically to all these responsibilities of the profession. Some will abhor assignments that require frequent committee meetings to deal with a personnel matter, though they may jump at the chance to initiate a project in which they can bring their own academic expertise to bear. (I recall just such an initiative from relevant faculty experts in creating a plan for the recycling of paper and other refuse at my own university.) It is a prime responsibility of those who become leaders in their own faculty senates to know the diverse capabilities of their faculties and be able to energize appropriate people for appropriate tasks.

American colleges and universities are not likely to develop governing councils on the British and Canadian model, in which a small number of faculty members sit with administrators and other designated officials to govern the institution. Whether or not it appears anomalous to those of us who are professional educators, our academic institutions will continue to invest ultimate decision-making authority in boards of trustees composed almost exclusively of nonacademics—whether businesspersons, public officials, or alumni—for whom running the institution is very much a part-time job.

Yet it is because they are not educational professionals themselves that boards made up of such individuals may be expected to assert their own power in fairly narrow terms. In general, that means that the financial health of the institution will be their core concern as long as the academic sector—including its administrative leadership—is acting responsibly in advancing the educational mission. Where a faculty is confident of the congruence between its professional values and the institution's mission, it will find that power and additional authority accrue to it.

It is another truism to note that the more prestigious the college or university, the greater the certainty that its faculty take seriously their professional responsibilities of the sort outlined above, and therefore exercise considerable authority in the governance of the institution. It is, not coincidentally, in these institutions that we expect the chief administrative officers to espouse and reflect these values in their own positions as well. Conversely, the farther down the status scale one goes, the greater the likelihood that the school will be run from the top down, with always visible and often conflict-ridden distinctions between its faculty and administrative sectors. There is where faculty members become mere employees and may lose sight of their professional responsibilities because they feel themselves denied true professional status.

So the road is hardest for faculties where a tradition of academic professionalism is largely unknown. There they may have to struggle to secure for themselves a place in governance that has long been assumed by their colleagues elsewhere. But until they are willing to make that effort, they deny their own professionalism and fail in some measure their calling.

This observation relates to the place of collective bargaining in higher education. It has proved to be a useful, probably even essential, tool for faculty rights on campuses where they have been least secure. Conversely, where a tradition of genuine faculty authority exists in governing the institution, unionization of the faculty generally has not occurred and presumably is not necessary.

The controversy over whether or not to unionize has largely centered around the question of whether or not it is antithetical to our professional role as "managers"—that is, as being centrally involved in setting educational priorities, maintaining standards, and engaging in all the other kinds of responsibilities discussed here. The decision in *NLRB* vs. *Yeshiva University* (444 U.S. 672) seemingly ruled that, for faculty in many private colleges and universities at least, the antithesis was real and unions could not be allowed. (One problem with the *Yeshiva* decision is that it evidently supported the rigidly class-based—and to my mind, reactionary—view that to engage in this kind of policy-making is to deny that one may also be an employee subject to the authority of others in such matters as salary and other benefits. The most enlightened current practice in the industrial sector increasingly includes employees in policy-making in order to secure the most productive results for the company.)

The usual criticism of *Yeshiva* from those who support collective bargaining for faculty is that it erroneously supposes that a faculty's role in such matters as curriculum planning or tenure and promotion means that the faculty share in policy-making, when in fact, according to this argument, their role is merely advisory.

To make explicit what I have been preaching here, I take the position that such an argument becomes self-defeating for any faculty, even where a factual case can be made for it. Our professional authority is, or ought to be, so evident to all as to be virtually unchallengeable from those outside the profession. Where that is the case, it is irrelevant whether our institutional charter proclaims our powers as only advisory or not, for in fact the faculty has important governmental powers. Where that is not the case, our only aim should be to assert the faculty's authority by exercising our professional responsibilities.

The one real, if misconceived, danger in faculty unionization is that it may permit the administration to argue that, having made the choice to unionize, the faculty has abrogated any claim it may have had to a professional role in shared governance. "Now that you've chosen an industrial model," say the institution's officers, perhaps even explicitly, "you'll be treated like industrial workers, without a voice in policy-making." This is not only a retrogressive view of labor-management relations; it can do unimaginable damage to the institution and to higher education generally. Instead of pursuing so reactionary a self-fulfilling prophecy, such an administration would be far better advised to recognize that the faculty simply wear two different hats, one when they are bargaining collectively and another when engaged in self-governance and shared governance in the institution.

Both fears—from the faculty, that its managerial role is a sham, and from the administration, that a unionized faculty has abdicated all responsibility to manage—are exaggerated and simplistic. The evidence now seems clear that faculty unions have *not* replaced traditional modes of faculty governance, that in healthy institutions unionization has often stimulated stronger and more effective faculty senates once it became clear that the two organizations served different but compatible purposes.[7]

A deep faculty involvement in the governance of colleges and universities is no panacea for the problems faced by higher education, but without that involvement those problems will not be effectively addressed. As new forces impact upon higher education and reshape our academic institutions, it is more crucial than ever that we struggle to maintain and enhance the central role of faculty in the governance of our campuses.

Georges Clemenceau asserted that war was too important to be left to the generals. So is higher education too important to be left predominantly to academic administrators. Like generals, these officers must concentrate increasingly on winning diverse battles at the cost of keeping their eye on the overriding purpose of education for humankind. It is the faculty who are most responsible for holding firmly to that purpose so that it guides each step we take as professional educators and every action pursued by our institutions of higher learning.

NOTES

1. David Lewin, lecture on collective bargaining in higher education, Temple University, as reported in *Faculty Herald*, Apr. 3, 1987.

2. Rose-Marie Oster, "Developing Faculty Leadership: A Faculty Perspective," in Madeleine F. Green, ed., *Leaders for a New Era* (New York: American Council on Education–Macmillan, 1988), p. 90.

3. As Paul H. L. Walter put it, "it is only when we accept, and are seen to accept, the grave responsibilities that unite university teachers as professionals that we dare claim from the public those extraordinary rights which allow us to pursue our profession. Until the professoriate saw itself in these terms, it had no claim to tenure, academic freedom, or shared governance." See "The Professor as Specialist and Generalist," *Academe* Vol. 74, No. 3 (May–June 1988): 25.

4. Ernest L. Boyer, *College: the Undergraduate Experience in America,* The Carnegie Foundation for the Advancement of Teaching (New York: Harper & Row, 1987).

5. Phyllis Franklin, David Laurence, and Robert D. Denham, "When Solutions Become Problems: Taking a Stand on Part-Time Employment," *Academe* Vol. 74, No. 3 (May–June 1988): 15–19.

6. In an address at Temple University on Feb. 5, 1988, Irving J. Spitzberg, Jr., citing the work of Steven J. Diner, *A City and Its Universities: Public Policy in Chicago, 1892–1919* (Chapel Hill: University of North Carolina Press, 1980), emphasized the challenge and the creative potential available to academics within their own environments. He argued that the discipline of political science as practiced in America today reflects the particular response of, principally, Charles E. Merriam to the political life of the city in which he lived and taught during his career nearly a century ago at the University of Chicago. In Spitzberg's words, "the process of creating the discipline (of political science) was dramatically affected by the fact that the (academic) institution was located in Chicago."

7. See, e.g., Irwin H. Polishook and Robert M. Nielsen, "Governance, Faculty Unions, and the Changing Workplace," Chapter IX of this book.

Chapter

7

The Role of Faculty in Campus Governance
Patricia R. Plante

As novelists and other students of human behavior have observed repeatedly over the years, small rebellions and neglects and incidents often carry disproportionately large consequences. And only those who have never sat on the banks of a northern river in early spring, when the sudden and deafening loosening of ice succeeds a barely perceptible crack, find the phenomenon either unnatural or surprising.

In a contemporary college/university management world that takes great pride in its systems analyses, its financial forecastings, its marketing strategies, and its many other sophisticated modes of operation, a fissure, unresponsive to the ministrations of data bases and in any event often so small as to draw little notice, is ignored in favor of more immediately and obviously threatening structural defects. This cleft that under all but the best of economic and social conditions might well lead to eventual serious damage on any campus is the neglect of one aspect of faculty development, namely, the encouragement and support of faculty leadership. Administrators who defer maintenance in this area have chosen, often with indolence if not malice aforethought, to position their institutions in a danger zone.

In a world where intellectualism reigns with the approval of virtually everyone, any attempt to improve a condition or to reform a system begins not unexpectedly with theoretical discussions of meaning and informative gathering of data. Hence, now that the question of leadership in academe, for a variety of historical, sociological, and economical reasons, is drawing ever-increasing attention, the debate over definition of terms and analysis of inferences is gaining momentum. Such a pleasurable exercise threatens, however, to remain academic in its multiple senses. While one should examine with care the premises underlying all definitions of leadership and one should analyze with equal attention useful figures attesting to progress or lack thereof, one should also guard against substituting examination and analysis for thoughtful action.

Higher education's present love affair with data gathering is in some instances skirting numerology. Signs of data wallowing are everywhere. Some data, but for its entertainment value, are useless: 39.5 percent of all white male assistant registrars assumed this position at a median age of twenty-seven years and four months. Some data, in the leadership advice category, are annoyingly simplistic: five items to include in a letter of nonreappointment. As if leadership were not a complex human matter incorporating dreams and rituals and myths.

The only practical problem with a definition of leadership is the obligation some feel to reach consensus as to its precise meaning. The only real problem with the immediate initiation of efforts that would encourage its development is the tendency to wait for computer printouts to shore up decisions that are perfectly secure and freestanding to begin with. Administrators who have become convinced that the development of faculty leadership is an important element of faculty development and who wish to support its promotion need only agree that leaders in academe seek, most frequently without prompting, creative paths to excellence and persuade others to follow these paths with enthusiasm.

In some human endeavors, precision is simply not the queen of virtues. Many a poet who could not to anyone's satisfaction define poetry has nevertheless written memorable verse. So, too, faculty on campuses all over the United States are at this very moment leading decision-making without worrying about lines of authority or about flowcharts or about narrative descriptions or numerical assessment of responsibility. The task of immediate importance is to take more effective measures to encourage and to support all faculty who wish to participate in decision-making regarding all matters affecting a college or university's welfare to be able to do so with ease. Let the debates over the proper definition of leadership and over the interpretation of data surrounding positions of power run their parallel courses. But let us not delay acting until the discussions have ceased and the computers have turned their fickle attention elsewhere, for by that time everyone may have become too bored with the topic to care. Joseph Epstein has wisely reminded us that "Just as primitive societies have no knowledge of the concept of vulgarity or poor taste, neither, one gathers, do they have bores. You need to attain a certain level of civilization to develop serious bores."[1]

However, even with goodwill and clearheadedness and even after having set aside lexical games as frequently if not always unproductive and self-indulgent, obstacles to faculty leadership development are not easily overcome. Three are especially difficult to score against.

1. Ironically, the American Association of University Professors (AAUP) has, since 1940 when it issued its statement of principles on academic freedom and tenure, done such commendable work in promoting and defending the legitimate rights of faculty as the primary decision-makers in certain areas of the academic domain that professors have been encouraged to gallop freely in certain corrals and have been deterred from entering others without anyone objecting to the fencing. Thus are faculty on most campuses given considerable opportunity for leadership in matters that form the academic heart of the enterprise: decisions regarding appointment, nonreappointment, tenure, and promotion of colleagues; curriculum and graduation standards; conditions of employment such as work load and evaluation systems. However, few faculty, especially in large universities, are involved in formulating policies regarding matters that affect the lives of students outside the classroom and that help form the culture of a campus in fundamental ways: strategic planning for the entire institution; improvement of the physical plant; fund-raising and institutional advancement; student recruitment, financial aid, and retention; management of residence halls; preparation of presentations to the various governing boards, members of the legislature, and the community at large. In addition, and in this case in spite of the AAUP's 1972 policy on the role of faculty in budgetary matters, few but the highest level of administrators are given an opportunity to link the allocation of funds to principles that undergird an institution's mission statement.

As if agreeing that good fences did make good neighbors, administrators in many universities do not expect to find an alien faculty at budgetary hearings and strategic planning sessions, and in return they themselves avoid trespassing on faculty territory. As reported and regretted by Clark Kerr and others, many university presidents spend little time on academic affairs, and all in higher education could name even academic vice presidents and deans who survive by bowing excessively low before the territorial imperative.

Thus have certain areas on campuses come to be known as appropriate for managerial overseeing by an administration not intellectually prepared to advance the knowledge of plasma physics and other zones marked as elevated enough to merit the attention of those engaged in promoting the life of the mind. And thus also can such a division between administrators and faculty lead to a college or university's lack of inner consistency, for no meaningful all-inclusive planning in the complex social context of the 1980s and 1990s can take place while these fences are allowed to stand. The challenge of the demolition work will, of course, depend upon the type, the size, and even the location of a college or university.

Oscar Handlin, Carl M. Loeb University Professor at Harvard University, in perhaps an unintended salute to these forbidden border crossings, has recently reminded faculty that libraries are too important to leave to librarians, for "Since they usually count themselves as members of the administration, they tend to align themselves with presidents, deans and provosts and too readily acquiesce in budgetary constraints."[2]

2. A second significant obstacle to the development of faculty leadership clings with the tenacity of a barnacle to faculty self-image. Colleges and universities were not created for the purpose of being administered. After the financial forecasting, after the office automation, after the marketing plans, after all of that and so much more, everyone knows that the heart of the enterprise beats in the classrooms, laboratories, and libraries. Witness the number of deans who would return to teaching "if only one could." Academe still reveres the monk in his cell, bending over an illuminated manuscript, even if in pin-stripe suit he now jets across continents to conferences and seminars. One simply does not meet biologists and poets and anthropologists who began their professional lives yearning to write student retention plans. Many still reason that faculty members who lead campus efforts not tied to the strictly and narrowly academic are undercover administrators, and since administrators are not worthy of undue respect, faculty leadership development is viewed as an endeavor of questionable merit.

Three thousand one hundred "custom-made" mission statements to the contrary, a universal academic culture often dismisses traditional concepts of leadership as the domain of administrators who seek happiness through power. Faculty, on the other hand, paint self-portraits that reveal tolerant, independent, contemplative, self-directed types who are not easily influenced, who are as wise as anyone claiming unusual insight and perspicacity, and who are comfortable in a slightly anarchical world. Not a one would trade a good infielder for an excellent manager.

3. An administrator whose aim to include faculty in all serious decision-making is not deflected by the artificial distinction between those areas within the academy that properly belong to the faculty and those that are the property of managers; an administrator who is not deterred from developing leadership from a faculty that holds a slight disdain for academic presidents, deans, and assorted acolytes is rewarded by having to find a hole through yet another wall.

Though a number of faculty and sympathetic administrators insist that the family quarrel between teaching and research is still at its height, and though some academic writers continue to give family counseling, many a campus is at peace with the issue—or, at least, has found peaceful if not perfect means of ending a debate that has gone on too long.

The culture of the academy is now such that many faculty in all types of higher education institutions have come to agree that their teaching should not be limited to the teaching of those who have registered for their courses, but that it must extend to teaching all those interested in their disciplines. Scholarship may be more broadly defined in one university than another, but faculty everywhere are persuaded that their teaching should not be fenced in by the borders of their classrooms and laboratories and that they should expose their views and conclusions to the critical review of peers from institutions other than their own.

More and more faculty in more and more colleges and universities with a modified but nevertheless approximate culture of the research university feel that their primary responsibility is to their discipline and that they best serve their home institution and its students by concentrating on their teaching and scholarship. Consequently, time given to long hours of committee work in support of shared governance is seen quite literally as "given."

Hence, the challenge for an administrator is to create a campus climate that encourages a giving that is generous and free, as opposed to one that is niggardly and conscripted. The campus culture should persuade as many faculty as possible that carrying a portion of the weight of shared governance is not only a noble enterprise but a civic obligation that one meets as conscientiously as one prepares intellectually worthwhile classes and manuscripts.

Consequently, a president, a provost, or a dean who sincerely wishes to pay more than lip service to the notion of shared governance and who is philosophically convinced that lines of authority in academe are appropriately lines of persuasion, must go over, under, or around the three major obstacles described above. The way to begin is by *not* engaging in certain behavior patterns that have traditionally camouflaged authoritarian intents even from those who practice them with what they believe are pure motives.

Faculty should never be asked to undertake clerical duties that can be done by staff.

Administrators in their salad days often mistakenly attempt to involve faculty in certain campus projects by asking them to perform undemanding tasks that teach little and that provide even less opportunity for decision-making. Experience should quickly teach them, if some historian or philosopher does not reach them even more quickly, that one who respects the importance of faculty teaching and scholarship does not interrupt either frivolously. However, when such requests are prompted not by inexperience and misguided goodwill but by a desire to appear to want to share power in a world that does not take kindly to autocracy, the action is dishonest as well as unwise. No one will long be deceived by an administrator who unilaterally decides what departments will be allotted additional faculty positions but is open to sharing the task of examining transcripts to be certain that seniors have met all graduation requirements. Faculty will respond generously when given an opportunity to seek solutions to problems worthy of their considerable talent and expertise, but they will justifiably resent the time stolen from their studies and their students for matters that might well be handled by staff. No one should confuse busy work with the acquisition of knowledge, including the knowledge of leadership.

Faculty should never be asked to attend meetings that have no specific and vital purpose.

Faculty who are serious about their own intellectual growth and that of their students do not need recreational directors. And it is patronizing to conclude that they will be flattered when invited to attend meetings whose purpose is neither to share significant information nor to reach a decision regarding a matter of some importance. To one who nurtures contemplative leanings, as many faculty do, no sense of self-worth is enhanced and no feeling of membership in a serious enterprise is promoted when one is asked to interrupt work on a manuscript or on class preparation to join administrators who are acting out of heavy-handed good intentions or, worse yet, are making a calculated attempt to appear open and nonautocratic, and so think it "time to touch base with the faculty." These shaggy-dog assemblies, like shaggy-dog stories, lead nowhere but to a sense that somehow one has missed the point. Surely, leading colleges and universities through the difficult and complex 1980s and 1990s cannot consist of trivializing questions while drinking cups of Maxwell House.

After attending a number of such gatherings, faculty who may have started out wishing to participate in shared governance react in predictable fashion. Some pay the same attention to future invitations as they do to junk mail; some lose confidence in the administrators who host these get-togethers and become increasingly anxious; some, long attached to the institution, continue to attend, but become ever more impatient and contentious; and, finally, some come to view the campus as simply a pied-à-terre that allows them certain comforts and privileges when they are in town.

Faculty should never be arbitrarily denied entrance into any area of decision-making.

Just as presidents, provosts, and deans should never conclude that academic decisions belong exclusively to the faculty, so too should they never designate fiscal affairs, university advancement, or any of the multiple support services areas as nontrespassing zones. It matters a great deal in strategic planning, that is, in the most effective use of an institution's resources for the purpose of attaining its dreams, to be certain, say, that courses are not duplicated in the departments of Management and Computer and Information Sciences, or in those of Sociology and Anthropology and History. An academic vice president or a dean should be knowledgeable enough to recognize excess and brave enough to discourage it. Similarly, policies, say, governing financial aid, faculty-student ratios, allocation of discretionary funds, priorities in capital projects, and much more have a significant and long-term impact on a college or university. Faculty should be given opportunities to remain informed and to express opinions on all matters that affect their lives and those of their students.

Clearly, faculty should not be asked to prepare requests to allow companies to bid to replace roofs and boilers. However, some well-intended efforts regarding certain aspects of campus life that might at first blush seem to belong exclusively to one division may upon reflection affect many who will understandably resent having to cope with consequences not of their making. Take the following instance.

The Personnel Department in a medium-size public university, exasperated by a seemingly unending flow of demands for the upgrading of secretarial positions in academic departments, obtains permission from the administrative vice president to impose a moratorium on all promotions of secretaries and to begin a thorough study of their duties and responsibilities. The undertaking is to include desk audits. The chairs of the forty departments and the faculty are informed, but not consulted. The initiative is to begin in January, and the results are to be made known in early spring. No one objects: a sizable majority, convinced that their secretary is superior to all other secretaries and remembering with gratitude the nights she worked overtime to meet grant application deadlines, anticipate the long overdue correction of an injustice; the others dismiss the project as another instance of pop management.

The exercise concludes in mid-April, and the members of the Personnel Department, having sincerely and conscientiously made every effort to remain objective and just, are astonished to discover that the faculty response might not have differed had they planted explosives in the campanile. Their announcement of the study's conservative conclusions during spring break is viewed as a cowardly administrative ploy to perform a dastardly deed while the faculty is away; their point system, which keeps virtually every secretary in situ for life, is indefensible and evidence of both simplemindedness and pettiness; their descriptive justifications support nothing but the well-known fact that the new breed of campus administrator understands nothing about the culture of academe and the needs of professors.

The vice president for administration hopes that we pass this way but once; the personnel officers busily defend themselves; the secretaries weep and threaten to leave; and the chairs and faculty write letters of outrage that demand immediate action from the provost and the president. One is reminded of a cartoon by Sempé that appeared in the *New Yorker* some years back. In what is clearly the last scene of a grand opera, the hero is collapsing at the feet of the dying heroine while light from a small gothic window illuminates a scene of general desolation. A bejeweled dowager in the audience turns to her companion and whispers: "What a shame! With a little professional help early on, all this could have been avoided." Well in this instance, perhaps not all, but anyone with an understanding of shared governance that wisely involves its faculty in the solution of problems, could most certainly have avoided some of the unfortunate consequences of what began as a project conceived as the exclusive domain of one division.

Faculty should never be forced to participate in an administration's plans to promote faculty leadership.

To insist that someone "lead" is about as reasonable as to insist that someone be charming. Leadership supposes self-propulsion. However, what administrators might well do is to encourage flight and to properly maintain the runways while ever keeping in mind that many may simply not be interested in traveling. To assume that a faculty member who turns down an opportunity to add to his or her leadership experience by chairing the university senate or by directing the business outreach program is alienated or uncaring or lazy or filled with self-doubt is presumptuous. Faculty who are happy as scholar-teachers and who carry their fair share of a campus community's civic obligations must be allowed their own Waldens.

Ironically, some administrators, in their eagerness to prove themselves egalitarians, unconsciously use their power of office to impose decision-making on some who have chosen the academic life precisely because they find management in all its forms uncongenial and contemplation in all its manifestations attractive. These same administrators, in their real or imagined desire to share power, not only frequently create the impression that no one is at the helm but, what is perhaps even worse, give signs of having little respect for the important calling of a scholar/teacher. These administrators find it beyond imagining that all faculty are not waiting to be "elevated" to the role of a dean or vice president, and are not eager to be provided with experiences that might eventually place them on those summits.

Formal leadership development efforts such as the American Council on Education's Fellows Program in Academic Administration and the Summer Institute for Women in Higher Education Administration at Bryn Mawr may be useful and perhaps even invaluable for faculty who wish to become deans and vice presidents. However, the end of faculty leadership development is not the transformation of faculty into administrators, and one should examine closely a rhetoric that implies values inimical to the primary mission of any college or university: to discover, to preserve, and to share knowledge and wisdom. Faculty who decide to seek administrative posts are not "moving up" or positioning themselves for "career advancement," though they may well be eager for a change of responsibilities.

In providing campus-based faculty development leadership opportunities, administrators must forever keep in mind the central purpose of such efforts and the philosophical conviction that gives it form. The aim is not to metamorphose physicists and literary analysts into deans and development officers, but to share with them a vision of their institution's destination and to search with them for the most honest and most honorable routes to travel by.

Assuming that one respects the central role of the faculty on any campus by not engaging them in clerical duties disguised as leadership assignments; by not interrupting their important work with trivial meetings meant to lead to no exit; by not excluding them from any realm of significant decision-making; and by not, through word or deed, implying that the good the brave and the beautiful leave small offices for larger ones, how is the faculty leadership voice amplified?

Though presidents, academic vice presidents, and deans must be allowed their style, it is difficult to imagine any of these administrators persuading a faculty that they subscribe to the importance of shared governance without three elements forming part of their mode of operation. Administrators who sincerely wish to promote faculty leadership development keep their faculty well informed; seek their faculty's advice on all significant issues, especially those involving personnel and fiscal matters; and use their faculty's initiatives as part of the institution's strategic planning.

Just as a scientist's years of advance study prepare him or her not only to detect the unusual but to deal with the previously unknown when it appears, so too a well-informed faculty is able to respond intelligently and wisely to the vagaries of fortune and the changing economic, political, and social influences that constitute a college or university's varied challenges. The ability to adapt is one of the virtues most needed in the complex world of contemporary higher education, but a faculty that is not prepared to anticipate change will greet it with defensiveness and hostility.

The tone with which administrators share information with faculty cannot be divorced from the information itself when discussing the benefits that accrue in such an educational process. It is essential that this tone be characterized by honesty and openness, of course, but just as importantly it must convey the conviction that the challenges to be met are not the property of the administration alone or of the faculty alone, but of the institution to which everyone belongs.

For instance, take the following account, in which details have been changed to protect those involved and a few facts have been altered to underscore a point but the essence of the story remains intact. In the early 1980s, an academic vice president in a state university with severely limited resources become convinced that the mounting of a graduate degree in Policy Studies would benefit both his institution and his community. With barely a nod to the principles of strategic planning and with close to universal indifference on the part of a faculty removed from serious decision-making and accustomed, if not resigned, to ad hoc actions from inexperienced though well-meaning academic officers, the vice president blithely instituted the program. Furthermore, he structured the program as freestanding—unattached to any college within the university.

On the day of the happy announcement, the sun shone for the last time. Storms that easily could have been forecasted came in quick succession and never abated. In an institution without a national reputation, the recruitment of students was appropriately confined to the immediate geographical area. The net for faculty was spread from coast to coast, but it caught many whose expectations both for salary and working conditions the university could not meet and many who were marginally qualified and/or talented. Directors came and went, carrying with them all of the baggage that had prevented them from running a successful race elsewhere.

From the opening term, the students within the program had expressed some disappointment with both the curriculum and the inappropriately low level of discourse in some of the classes. After five years of patiently waiting and hoping both for quality and stability, a significant number of the often good and nearly always older and place-bound students began to threaten to expose what they perceived to be a shoddy degree program now administered by this director, now by that one.

In an effort at damage control, the beleaguered program director of the moment began to offer additional monetary compensation to strong faculty from various appropriate departments (Economics,

Political Science, Management Studies) as incentives to teach in the Policy Studies Program. The vice president for academic affairs, not known for his management skills and given to reacting defensively at every opportunity, "discovered" the offers only after understandings were reached between the director of the program and several faculty members. At this point, the vice president, while assuming no responsibility for having been unaware of this model of an entrepreneurial spirit, declared all of the understandings null and void. The reaction from the faculty involved and from all sympathizing colleagues was predictably one of outrage and bitterness, and a program that had never walked with purpose was about to find it difficult to crawl.

That this mini–case study illustrates any number of leadership and managerial weaknesses goes without saying, but one of the most egregious is the nearly total lack of understanding of the proper role of faculty leadership in a university. To imagine that one can mount a successful and stable academic program without widespread faculty guidance, support, and involvement in its every aspect and at its every stage of development is at best naive and at worst arrogant.

Most often when making decisions in an academic culture, one's only meaningful choice of style is to devote time in involving others, particularly faculty, before or after the deed. The administrator as teacher never begrudges the hours spent sharing knowledge with and listening to the suggestions of faculty before reaching decisions. He or she does so willingly not only because such is the only viable way to create a climate of shared purpose, not only because faculty are among the most intelligent and best-trained people in society who can make significant contributions to the leadership of an institution, but because the hours not spent educating and listening before acting are going to be spent with interest after acting. The explanations and justifications that follow a decision for which a faculty had never been prepared and to which it had never been asked to contribute will always ring hollow regardless of the acoustics.

Very specific occasions that afford administrators opportunities to encourage faculty leadership in many spheres of college or university life are those that appear as requests to support faculty initiatives. While the generous cheer on the worthy projects of others, nearly everyone reserves a special enthusiasm and affection for those ventures born of their own minds and hearts. Hence, administrators who are not inclined to censure that aspect of human nature are in a better position to work it to the benefit of their institution as well as to the benefit of the faculty who ask to launch new satellites.

Consider, for instance, the case of Professor A, a physicist of considerable talent who has the respect of both his colleagues and his students and who was suddenly awakened to the anorexic condition of the university's centralized academic advising system by the noise and confusion surrounding the implementation of computerized registration. The dean and the provost, both convinced that Professor A did not mean to limit his concern to lamentations in the faculty dining room, met with him in order to seek his help in improving a system that they acknowledged to be weak. They granted him a reduced teaching load and funds to attend national conferences that featured successful academic advising programs in return for his leading the faculty in his college in the designing of a more effective student advising system. They made certain that the staff in the centralized Office of Advising supported his efforts and did not interpret them as interference, and an enthusiastic Professor A now plans a study of the benefits of computer-assisted advising programs that are operative at Brigham Young University and elsewhere. The improvements made in his college will be studied in the other divisions of the university for possible implementation. A fine physicist and teacher was not transformed into an administrator; a fine faculty member was given the opportunity to help lead a university toward excellence.

Genuine efforts on the part of administrators to share the governance of a college or university with the faculty will not relieve presidents, provosts, and deans of assuming the ultimate responsibility for decisions that define and direct an institution. Sincere attempts to develop faculty leadership will not guarantee consensus on all issues. Indeed, there will be times when an administrator will conclude that the majority voice, while the strongest, is not the purest. However, a faculty that is persuaded of the authenticity of an administration's desire to include others in its decision-making is a faculty that will generously respect, even support, conclusions that differ from their own.

In a 1936 letter to Elizabeth Ames, the Director of Yadoo, novelist John Cheever wrote that an old lady in his Washington, D.C., boardinghouse claimed that all WPA workers were lazy and generally good for nothing. Cheever was finding it harder and harder "to pass her the lima beans." Administrators and faculty who are sensitive to the complexitites of leading colleges and universities through the 1980' and 1990's are finding it harder and harder to respond amicably to those in positions of power who seem unaware that the neglect of the development of faculty leadership is a fissure in an institution of higher education that might well signal the eventual disintegration of a united undertaking.

NOTES

1. "The Bore Wars," *The American Scholar* 56 (Winter 1987): 24.
2. *The American Scholar* 56 (Spring 1987): 218.

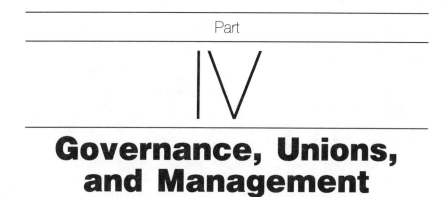

Part

IV

Governance, Unions, and Management

In the 1960s, the establishment of faculty unions on a number of campuses seemed to challenge traditional modes of faculty governance, not to mention traditional expectations as to how governance of the institution was shared. Although collective bargaining unquestionably has had an impact on the way many academic institutions are run, its history has unfolded differently from what might have been anticipated: unionization has constituted only one, and frequently not the most consequential, challenge to established patterns of governance on American campuses since the 1960s. That is a major theme throughout Chapter 8. Second, where they have coexisted, collective bargaining and more traditional faculty governance processes have tended toward mutual accommodation rather than conflict, which in turn has led to the kind of creativity analyzed and advanced in Chapter 9.

George Keller argues in Chapter 8 that the United States is now at its third historic watershed in the history of academic participation in campus governance. Yet that is less the result of the impact of faculty unionization (which does not even enter into Keller's analysis) than of a whole range of societal trends that are, for the most part, well beyond the control of the campus. He discerns the emergence of novel governance forms as a response, forms which, in his view, attempt to eschew the inherently *political* structures of divided power and authority for the *managerial* decision-making techniques that combine them. He contends, too, that the political approach of shared governance is inherently conservative, while emerging forms of campus management may represent an ability for decision-makers to act more quickly and decisively in response to new demands.

In Chapter 9, Irwin H. Polishook and Robert M. Nielsen focus on collective bargaining for faculty in higher education by way of examining changes in labor-management relations throughout society. They contend that the experience of shared faculty responsibilities in academic unions and faculty senates is an accomplished fact on many campuses today and may now become a quasi-model for greater labor-management cooperation elsewhere in the marketplace. Noting that increased professionalization of the work force is a trend already well under way in postindustrial societies, they view the amalgam of faculty governance and collective bargaining as having established an "effective working model that bridges the gap between . . . industrial model bargaining . . . and a modern, cooperatively managed workplace."

The development of grievance systems has been one of the most noteworthy additions to faculty governance with the creation of faculty unions. Barbara Lee notes, as the premise of Chapter 10, that grievance systems for faculty in colleges and universities have been assumed to be good, and that there has been no evaluation of their worth in the literature on higher education. She proceeds to her own evaluation, finding both boons and banes in the ways in which they work. Her concluding, cautionary note warns against the temptation to let grievance issues fill up the whole agenda of faculty governance, crowding out other matters in which faculties must remain involved.

Shotgun Marriage
The Growing Connection Between Academic Management and Faculty Governance

George Keller

In the 1980s, the faculty's role in governing U.S. colleges and universities has been going through a remarkable transformation. Something new is emerging, the exact outlines of which are still unclear. But what is clear is that the "unique dualism"[1] that has characterized university administration in the post–World War II period is crumbling, and new forms of academic management are being tried.

A shift of governance has happened twice before. In the earliest days of U.S. colleges, the trustees usually dominated matters of policy, instruction, discipline, and facility construction and use. But in the late nineteenth century, as higher education moved from tiny, religious schools to state universities, great private universities, and larger secular colleges, the presidents took over as executives of change and master builders: "captains of erudition," Thorstein Veblen called them. There were few faculty meetings, and as one researcher noted, "The faculty in the early American university felt no strong desire to manage their institutions."[2] Eliphalet Nott, president of New York's Union College from 1804 to 1866, said about faculty meetings late in his career, "I remember having one once, some thirty-six years ago, but I never wish to have another."[3]

After the founding of the American Association of University Professors (AAUP) in 1915, the second shift occurred. The faculty slowly began to assert the idea of shared governance with the president. At first, professors were restrained and cautious. Committee T (on the Place and Function of Faculties in University Government and Administration) of the AAUP wrote in its famous 1920 report:

> The chief objections urged against . . . thoroughgoing faculty autonomy in university government are as follows: the lack of concentration of authority and responsibility would conduce to inefficiency; there would be a lack of initiative and leadership; personalities and politics would play too large a part in university government and administration; members of the faculty would spend too much of their time in the details of administration and executive work. . . . A university needs *leadership* in its presiding officers.[4]

However, the AAUP leaders did assert, "In the matter of the determination and carrying out of educational policies, the members of the faculty are the experts, and should have the principal voice in the decision."[5]

By the 1960s, faculty power had become so great that McGeorge Bundy could write, "When it comes to a crunch, in a first-class university it is the faculty which decides."[6] And Columbia sociologist Paul Lazarsfeld worried, "We witness a dangerous divergence. Academic freedom is more and more interpreted in such a way as to keep the administration out of any truly academic affairs. . . . But educational innovations are by definition intellectual as well as administrative tasks. And so, they have fallen into a no-man's. . . . As a result, many of our universities have a dangerously low level of organizational development."[7] The low level of institutional development was exacerbated too by the sudden rise of faculty unionism in the 1960s among community and state colleges.

By the late 1970s, many colleges and universities had reached an impasse in management and governance, especially since the ideology and rhetoric of faculty power remained while the reality of faculty governance disintegrated. The increasing size of the faculties, the growing specialization of university life, and the orientation of more scholars to their professional fields rather than to their own campus combined to break collegiality into shards. And the growing financial difficulties and retrenchment of the 1970s made faculty governance an exceedingly unpleasant activity. By 1980, numerous faculty senates could no longer muster a quorum. "In most of our large institutions there are few evidences of an academic community," T. R. McConnell observed.[8]

At the same time that faculty enthusiasm for campus policy-making was dissolving, the United States entered a new era in which unprecedented developments in society required colleges and universities to act more swiftly in educational policy changes, hard decisions, and institutional renovation. It was this clash between the urgent new need for university change and the stymied, shattered forms of shared governance that led to American higher education's third major shift. Academic governance and management began trying new patterns and experimenting with novel kinds of campus decision-making. In the late 1980s, Americans are at a watershed in the history of academic participation in the direction of our universities.

Changes Forcing New Governance

Colleges and universities have always been buffeted by outside forces, but seldom so much as at the present time. The external conditions on which college policy is based are changing with astonishing speed.

Demographically, there is the well-known decline in births that will reduce the number of high-school graduates by one-fourth between 1979 and 1995. Already more than one-fourth of America's colleges and some universities have reduced enrollments. There is the explosion in immigration, especially from Latin America and Asia, that is altering the ethnic composition and educational focus of many institutions. And there is the aging of U.S. society. One-eighth of the nation's population is over sixty-five. By the year 2020, this will rise to nearly one-fifth. Increasing numbers are enrolling in higher education, forcing changes in pedagogy, scheduling, and course content.

Economically, the thirty years of unrivaled prosperity from 1945 to 1974 are over. The United States now faces fierce competition, the loss of manufacturing and agricultural jobs to countries abroad, and mounting national deficits. As a result, enrollments in business courses are ballooning, and many universities are being beseeched to help with their state's or region's economic stability and development. Because U.S. trade with Asia is increasing, colleges are compelled to become less Eurocentric in their focus and to turn their attention to Asian culture, economics, language, and politics.

The years of government largesse are past; yet higher education costs are rising 30 percent faster than the cost-of-living index.

Socially, the nation is going through an erosion of the nuclear family. The number of one-parent families has risen from 7.4 percent in 1950 to 28 percent in 1987. Teenage pregnancies have reached epidemic proportions. This change has caused disorder and lack of motivation for study to become major new problems in the schools. It is also forcing expensive new programs in tutoring, counseling, and special student activities on most campuses.

America's black population is polarizing, as more educated blacks assume positions of importance and the number of undereducated, unruly blacks becomes what even black scholars admit is an "underclass." Last year, two-thirds of all black children were born out of wedlock, and the number of blacks applying for college is declining. In Virginia, for example, only 2,000 of the 12,000 black high-school graduates take college-preparatory programs. Institutions committed to affirmative action are being compelled to rethink their efforts.

Technologically, we have burst into a new age of computers and telecommunications. This is altering not only university pedagogy and research but also the connections among colleges and between the campus and museums, corporations, government agencies, and other institutions.

Last, there are the changes in students and in faculty. In 1987, 43 percent of the 12 million students enrolled in higher education were over twenty-five years of age. Fewer than one-sixth of all students are full-time, residential enrollees. As for the faculty, they are getting older as a group, and perhaps one-fourth will retire in the coming decade. One-third of all U.S. faculty are now part-time appointments. One-fourth belong to faculty unions.

When these seismic shifts are combined, the impact is huge. Colleges and universities need to adapt, to respond, to redesign their operations, and each campus needs to clarify its particular role in the higher education network of thirty-two hundred institutions. The demand for strong, decisive action in academe is growing. The need for vigorous, strategic management at each college and university has become imperative. Yet, most institutions have proud but relatively inactive, fearful, and unenterprising faculty governments and highly deferential, cagey, and timorous presidents, provosts, and deans. Just when historical conditions require stronger executive leadership in academe, the governance and management of many U.S. colleges and universities are in disarray.[9]

Out of Necessity, New Forms of Governance

In any enterprise, when goals cannot be clearly defined or the need for swift adaptation is urgent, the demand for leadership increases enormously.[10] This is what is happening in higher education. Institutions must decide what to do about enrollments, technology, the orient, minorities, weaker student preparation, aging scientific equipment, serious financial squeezes, and other matters. So a small but growing number of colleges and universities are creating new, action-oriented, decision-ready structures of governance.

No one model has emerged as the new form of governance for the 1990s. But based on my work from 1982 to 1988 as a higher education consultant, and on my inquiries and quasi-research, I suspect that many of the new adventures in governance are tending toward what might be called the Joint Big Decisions Committee. That is, top college administrators and leading faculty are combining their efforts in a new kind of cabinet government—a novel, joint, policy-making committee that advises on the priorities for action, educational focus, and expenditures for the institution. It is variously named the Budget and Priorities Committee, the President's Advisory Committee, or some similar name. But its ingredients are becoming clear.

Instead of the old Faculty Senate and the president's cabinet meeting separately, a select number from both meet together. Instead of educational policy and institutional and financial policy being decided separately, they are decided in tandem. The AAUP idea of education decisions being made by the faculty in isolation from money, enrollments, or the overall strategies of the institution increasingly seems naive. Instead of planning disconnected to the annual budget, ideas and financial support for them are linked. Budgets follow strategies more and more instead of following territorial claims. And instead of decisions based on the needs of units or departments, they are increasingly based on the health and direction of the entire college or university.

Obviously, the growth of these new faculty-administration policy groups has been easier to assemble at smaller institutions such as Indiana's Depauw University, Austin Community College in Texas, or Tennessee's Carson-Newman College. But universities such as Princeton and the University of Miami have also succeeded in assembling these new governance forms.

Both professors and administrators have had to change their modes of operation. The president, financial vice president, and provost—and the athletic director—have had to be more open about the budget and their priorities for the future. They have had to respect faculty opinion more deeply and tolerate controversy, disagreement, and conflict more patiently. Faculty members, usually elected, have had to move beyond their own craft guild concerns, to honor confidences, and to make difficult, painful decisions. Some committees have had stormy voyages; a few others have grown into powerful bodies recommending each year what the college or university should be doing for the next five to seven years.

Moving Beyond Governance

One of the radical implications of these emerging new forms of campus management is questioning the idea of governance itself as an appropriate activity at a college or university. Governance is a *political* activity. It assumes that a university is a primarily political institution, with a separation of powers between the faculty and the administration, and with politically constituted committees as a major source of university policy. But multi-interest politics, we are discovering, is inherently conservative, and campus politics often renders a university unable to act in the face of rapidly changing and potentially threatening conditions. Political governance tends to focus on competitor groups internally, and tends to prevent unified or collaborative action against external competitors or hostile forces. As some small colleges battle for survival, and as larger institutions seek to prevent retrenchment or a decline in quality and level of financial support and public service, political infighting may need to be complemented with stronger (but representative) management of the whole institution. The future of the college or university as an entity appears to be taking precedence over the special interests of departments or schools.

Thus, what is emerging is some fresh kind of higher education *management*—a management committee that includes elected faculty and selected administrators (and sometimes a student or two, a staff person, or a trustee). But this new management is to some extent politically grounded. Both governance and routine administration are being superseded by pressing demands to reshape the modern university and college to meet a new external environment.

Good-bye to Uniformity in Governance

One probable result of this third major change in U.S. university governance is the end of uniform governance patterns. There always were variations, of course; but from now on it is likely that the way institutions are run will vary considerably. The old AAUP prescriptions will be increasingly difficult to adhere to. America's higher education institutions are becoming more varied as they compete for a declining pool of traditional students and a more diverse pool of new students. Since the late 1960s, the advent of faculty unions at community colleges, state colleges, and some public and private universities is also adding to the variety of governance-management schemes in the academic world.

Each college and university will increasingly be pushed to find its own way to merge traditional faculty governance and new academic management. Each will need to look more intensely at its own traditions, patterns of operation, institutional culture, administrative history, and degree of faculty participation, as well as to its own requirements for leadership in order to meet changing conditions, declining resources, and new demands for intellectual service from the public and its leaders.

NOTES

1. John J. Corson, *Governance of Colleges and Universities* (New York: McGraw-Hill, 1960), p. 43.

2. Walter Schenkel, "Who Has Been in Power?" in Harold Hodgkinson and L. Richard Meeth (eds.), *Power and Authority: Transformation of Campus Governance* (San Francisco: Jossey-Bass, 1971), p. 16.

3. Timothy Dwight, *Memories of Yale Life and Men* (New York: Dodd, Mead, 1903), p. 110.

4. Committee T, "Report on the Place and Function of Faculties in University, Government and Administration," *AAUP Bulletin* 6 (March 1920): 24.

5. *Ibid.*, p. 25.

6. McGeorge Bundy, "Faculty Power," *Atlantic Monthly* (September 1968).

7. Paul Lazarsfeld and Sam Sieber, *Organizing Educational Research* (Englewood Cliffs, N.J.: Prentice-Hall, 1964), p. 13.

8. T. R. McConnell, "Faculty Government" in Hodgkinson and Meeth, *Power and Authority*, p. 100.

9. George Keller, *Academic Strategy: The Management Revolution in American Higher Education* (Baltimore: Johns Hopkins University Press, 1983).

10. Philip Selznick, *Leadership in Administration* (Evanston: Row, Peterson, 1957), p. 16.

9

Governance, Faculty Unions, and the Changing Workplace

Irwin H. Polishook and Robert M. Nielsen

As our nation's economy continues its shift from industrial manufacturing to information processing, two major trends are emerging within the worlds of work and learning. The first is that higher education is rapidly becoming a basic industry, playing much the same role with respect to the information economy as steel and coal once did for the old manufacturing industries. The second is the thrust among all sectors of the economy for greater labor-management cooperation, that is, toward establishing more collaborative, less adversarial, less confrontational relations as a means toward a more productive and competitive economy.

There is a chain of connection between these two trends. For example, the organization and self-governance of the campus academic community strongly resemble an ideal form of many recent industrial sector experiments with employee self-management and decentralized decision-making models. Technological advances have changed the very nature of work itself, requiring a more autonomous, creative, highly educated, and skilled employee. At the same time, research shows there has been a fundamental change in the job expectations of the American worker. Unlike the vast majority of workers a generation ago, who found work a necessary sacrifice for the well-being of their families, today's employees are far more likely to expect jobs to fulfill their personal needs for self-expression. In this regard, the "new workers" are not unlike their professorial counterparts, in the high skills levels required, the necessity for autonomy, and the desire for meaningful employment. Finally, the unique amalgamation of faculty-shared governance and collective bargaining in American higher education has established an effective working model that bridges the gap between rigid, two-sided industrial model bargaining as defined by the Wagner Act and a modern, cooperatively managed workplace.

The importance of these developments is underscored by the "competitiveness agenda," which is forging a consensus for labor-law reform in both the public and private sectors. This consensus is fueled by a growing awareness among labor, management, and government leaders that the old industrial assumptions—labor and management are two warring parties and government is a disinterested peacemaker—are no longer advantageous. Indeed, these concepts and practices are so out of step with the needs of a changing economy and the U.S. position in the global market as to be dangerous to our survival. Few specific reforms have been put forth as yet. But it is clear, nonetheless, that their formulation will be guided by the necessity for a new "alignment of interests" between employees and the corporations they work for, and that the realignment will be constrained to the extent that existing labor-management practice and precedent impede adjustments.

Higher Education and the New Work Ethic

The very idea of considering higher education in industrial terms grates harshly on academic ears, often calling forth allegations of sacrilege and heresy. Our modern community of scholars is more comfortable with medieval metaphors of Church and Guild—the rich symbolism of mortarboard, gown, hood, and mace—than the less-appealing images of production and commerce. Nonetheless, this is not eighteenth-century continental Europe, and like almost everything else here, institutions of higher learning have been shaped by our history. However nostalgic one might feel about the displacement of venerable old titles such as Leed's "Rector Magnificus" by its American counterpart, the more mundane president or chancellor, there is merit in describing our "system" of higher education as it actually is.

In many ways, higher education in the United States represents the very best of our democratic and economic traditions. Composed of over 3300 institutions of every shape and variety, it offers a mind-boggling array of educational programs and research services to consumers ranging from the richest business corporations and governmental agencies to students from the poorest segments of our socioeconomic spectrum. Collectively, these institutions are democratic in the scope of their offerings and the constituencies they serve. They are hierarchical in form and sometimes commercial in their market approach to attracting students. The American system of higher education, to the astonishment of most foreign observers, is perhaps characterized best by its lack of system. By sheer size alone, higher education constitutes a major U.S. industry, educating more than 12 million students, employing more than 2 million people, and generating revenues of close to $100 billion. In many cities, a college or a university is the largest single employer, as is the case with the University of Pittsburgh. In Washington, D.C., the fourteen institutions of higher education, considered as a whole, rank second only to the federal government in size, leaving tourism in the nation's "tourist capital" the district's third largest industry. Higher education performs more than 50 percent of the nation's basic research and serves another 20 million students through off-campus and extension programs. As an industry, it is larger than communications, petrochemicals, automobiles, or agriculture. If one counted the assets of physical plants, higher education nationally would probably rank second only to government in the extent of its operations. But it is the relationship of higher education to the new forces propelling economic growth that reinforces its role as an emerging basic industry.

The national economy is moving relentlessly from one anchored in the older, "smokestack" manufacturing industries to one grounded in high technology and based in the knowledge and service industries. This newest economy, the "information economy," is symbolized by the computer just as the factory and plow signified its industrial and agrarian predecessors. Coming with awesome and dramatic swiftness, this shift is transforming the nation.

Just as the change from an agricultural economy to an industrial economy required enormous adjustments in the educational requirements of the nation's work force, so too does the shift to an information economy. Because the time span of this current change is so shortened compared to past experience, demands on the education community are even more complicated; now the responsibility for retraining workers holding obsolescent jobs must be added to the challenge of educating the future work force. Equally important in expediting these changes is the partnership role with business and government that higher education must play in research and development efforts.

The increasing demand for higher education by the American work force is clearly visible. Already, a majority of the 115-million-member work force are in white-collar, technical, and professional jobs. The number of scientists and engineers in the American work force grew by 70 percent between just 1974 and 1986, the greatest increase in more than forty years. Today, there are more insurance workers than steelworkers, more teachers than construction workers, and more college professors than automobile workers. Or consider the massive shift in the work force in just two decades: in 1966, only one in every eight American workers had a college degree; in 1970, one in seven; and in 1986, one in four. Furthermore, the employment picture is evolving so rapidly that anyone entering the job market today is expected to change positions many times during a work life. The basic survival instincts of working men and women are evidenced by the fact that nearly 46 million adult Americans are engaged in a systematic way in some form of postsecondary education.

Not surprisingly, the impact of the new technologies has transformed the very nature of work itself, both in its application to existing industries and in newly created enterprises. In general, these alterations involve the elimination of many routine and purely manual tasks, vesting individual employees with a great deal more information about and control over production processes, and the generation of more interesting and creative work. In turn, these changes require greater autonomy and discretion on the part of the individual worker and alter the traditional function of middle management. A current aphorism asserting that "managing creativity is like trying to manage a butterfly" captures both the spirit and the necessity for the changes.

Recent experimentation with decentralized decision-making models of work organization and efforts to blur the distinctions between workers and managers are better understood in this context. Such highly touted General Motors–United Automobile Workers endeavors as the Saturn Project are good examples of the trend toward worker-manager collaboration in older industries. From another perspective, one might say that blue-collar work is becoming more technical and professional in nature, requiring many of the skills formerly associated only with white-collar, technical, and professional work. The "professionalization" of the workplace is, not unnaturally, accompanied also by the need for some employee involvement in corporate governance.

Concurrent with the rise of new work has been a dramatic change in the American work force—not merely in its level of expertise and educational achievement, but in the values people hold about work. A 1983 study by Daniel Yankelovich of the Public Agenda Foundation, *Putting the Work Ethic Back to Work,* strongly suggests that the work ethic is alive and well among both younger and older workers, but that it has changed in form. A typical worker of the previous generation possessed a work ethic grounded in the belief that work was a necessary sacrifice to be made for the benefit and well-being of the family. Indeed, it was a sacrifice made necessary by the fact that male heads of single-earner households composed 70 percent of the 1950s work force. By contrast, today 70 percent of the baby-boomer households have two wage earners, and they do not see work as synonymous with sacrifice, but rather as a form of "expressiveness."

This shift in values has generated what pollster Daniel Yankelovich calls a "huge rise in individualism in the workplace." It takes several forms. First, it has produced a highly competitive attitude among younger workers, who demand greater pay and more rapid advancement in return for higher performance. Second, jobs themselves have become a source of self-expression. Doing things, making things, being associated with products and services of quality are important to these new workers: "Quality is what I do. It expresses me. If the quality is junky, then it says something terrible about me and threatens my individuality." And finally, autonomy. The more discretion a worker has, the more control over one's work, the greater the sense of individualism. The challenge before us is to create possibilities for the fulfillment of these values rather than have them dissipated in the frustrations of tedium.

Yankelovich's research suggests that new work-ethic values represent a large and relatively untapped potential for increasing productivity to the levels necessary to make the American economy competitive in the world marketplace. However, "putting the work ethic back to work" involves disencumbering the workplace of the anachronisms of the old industrial factory system, a system largely divided into workers and bosses functioning within an authoritarian, hierarchical structure. It involves understanding that while mediocrity may be enforcible, excellence is not; that more is to be gained through cooperation than confrontation; and that an emphasis on "mutuality rather than militancy" will contribute to advancing a "new ordering of labor-management relations which aligns manager and worker on the same side—working together for the common good."

Recent survey research of both union and nonunion members, conducted for the AFL–CIO by Louis Harris Associates, further discloses some fresh insights into the attitudes of present-day American workers. Among the more notable findings were that a majority enjoyed their jobs, did not find the company that employed them a natural enemy, liked their bosses, desired a less adversarial means of solving work-related problems, and disapproved of a good many work rules—both company- and union-imposed—because they interfered with the efficient performance of their work.

From 1980 to 1988, the American Federation of Teachers has undertaken parallel studies of college and university faculty in conjunction with several large collective bargaining elections. This research, conducted by Peter Hart Associates and Louis Harris Associates, shows surprisingly strong similarities with the AFL–CIO results. Like their counterparts in other sectors of the economy, a majority of the professors esteem their work, institutions, and presidents. They are collegial to the core and inveterately opposed to bureaucratic rules and red tape.

Even while recognizing the presence of autocratic administrative structures and rule-making, faculty fear that collective bargaining will reduce collegiality. The margin of victory or defeat in a campus collective bargaining election is sometimes a measure of the faculty's understanding that academic unionism bears small resemblance to industrial-model bargaining, either in form or practice.

What is it about college professors and autoworkers that causes them to share similar attitudes about their work environment? Or is that even the right question? Perhaps it would be closer to the mark to ask, "What is it about the nature of their work that causes them to share these similarities?" In fact, both questions are relevant, but for different reasons. In the language of Daniel Yankelovich, it is the amount of discretion that plays a large part in shaping an employee's feeling about the job. It is also clear that the impact of technology on the industrial workplace is increasing the demand for yet more employee discretion.

The related question is autonomy. In the case of the professors, increased bureaucratization and managerial hierarchy have resulted from the increased size and complexity of higher education, as well as from escalating governmental regulations. These developments have diminished autonomy by eroding the mechanisms of shared governance, the vehicle through which autonomy is exercised. In the case of the industrial worker, autonomy is something new to the workplace and is a product of the decentralized and participatory decision-making models of industrial organization. If this analysis is pointed in the right direction, it strongly suggests that the new work ethic values appearing in Yankelovich's poll results are very much the same as those that have always been associated with self-governing professional employees. It also suggests that the relationship between faculty governance mechanisms and collective bargaining may yield valuable insights into how experiments in industrial participative decision-making ought to be structured in order to integrate employee autonomy and discretion into the corporate enterprise.

Learning from Faculty Collective Bargaining

The distinguishing feature of faculty collective bargaining is that it is less confrontational, less two-sided, and more cooperative than its industrial and public sector counterparts. In many ways it mirrors the current call by labor, business, and government leaders for greater labor-management cooperation. Why these differences? And can they be duplicated in other sectors?

The answers to these questions are not to be found in any examination of the actual processes of collective bargaining, for these are essentially neutral; their form and substance reflect the institutional structure of the employer and nature of management. Put another way, collective bargaining is interactive. A college faculty's relationship with its institution differs from the industrial employee-employer relationship in that it is consensual. It is founded in the traditional role of scholars in professional decision-making, and commonly given written expression in faculty handbooks and board of trustee bylaws. Within this well-established framework, professors attempt to exercise their autonomy and responsibilities as citizens of a community of scholars, using the instruments of shared governance.

A collateral effect of the enormous growth and complexity of American higher education since World War I has been the substitution of administrative-faculty control by managerial control.

One outcome of this process is that faculty-shared governance lost much of its authority; this is one of the dominant impressions of professors identified in virtually every higher education opinion survey. It suggests faculties have sought collective bargaining contracts as a means of strengthening and supplementing their governance rights in order to counterbalance the encroachment of increasing managerial prerogative.

The fact that faculty collective bargaining takes place within the context of a written, almost constitutional relationship accounts for the cooperative nature of its practices. Although reasons of collegiality and community may account for some degree of the more cooperative character of faculty collective bargaining, in the main, collaboration results from the multiplication of the possible means of problem-solving. It is difficult to conceive of a problem that would not legitimately fall within the mechanisms of collective bargaining or governance—indeed, the only real difficulty arises when an issue can legitimately be resolved in either one or both areas.

A derivative benefit of bargaining under the statutory protection of state or national laws that recognize the right of professors to form unions is that it gives the faculty external, legal authority to bolster its legitimate claim to share in the decision-making powers, often only loosely defined in campus governance documents. The employment relations law—whether the National Labor Relations Act (NLRA) or any of its state-public-employee counterparts—requires that the employer "negotiate in good faith" with employees through their representative organization and provides sanctions for not doing so.

The first and most important of these effects is the enhancement of both the quality and quantity of faculty governance. Faced with the alternative of dealing with an issue in good faith at the bargaining table, more often campus management will elect to use the mechanism of self-governance. Faculty committees that had been either ignored completely or dealt with, only in superficial and meaningless ways, if at all, suddenly find they have renewed authority. One of the ironies of faculty collective bargaining is that it has proven a great vehicle for instructing new college and university managers—often inexperienced in campus management or government—in the importance of the traditions and practices of consensually defined shared governance within an academic community.

A final, major collateral effect of the constitution/contract dialectic of faculty collective bargaining is that it works toward maintaining a "sense of community" in the face of managerial centralization, which pulls hard in the opposite direction. Without this unique combination of constitution and contract, there is little to prevent the polarization of the academic community into hostile camps, with the faculty alienated from institutional management and functioning as little more than "hired hands." Gone also would be any hope for that "alignment of interest" between the faculty and the institution that Supreme Court Justice William Powell found so necessary while denying professors the right to organize a union under the NLRA at Yeshiva University.

Improving the Future of Work

The problems confronting the United States as a result of the declining industrial and emerging information economies are difficult and complex, yet they are not unfamiliar within our national experience. What is new in the present situation is the rapidity of the change. Unlike the movement from an agrarian to an industrial economy, which took more than one hundred years to complete, the current shift will occur over a span of less than thirty years. In human terms, the potential consequences of this lightning pace are disrupted communities, dislocated families, and desolated lives. At the same time, this could be a period of great promise and opportunity, for less drudgery and boredom and less physically debilitating work, for opportunities to restructure the workplace and the corporation, for defining a new partnership between America's working men and women and the companies that employ them, for creating new labor-management relations—in short, the promise of a more meaningful, more satisfying work life.

Our solutions must respond to this duality of hope and despair. The periodic and systematic economic pillaging of our cities and states, while merely offering the expectation of a brighter future for an elite few, is no longer tolerable. Nor is it enough to eliminate executive privileges and blur distinctions between workers and managers, or any of the other half-dozen cosmetic and paternalistic mutations designed to create an American version of the Japanese workplace. It is insufficient to retrain displaced autoworkers as word processors or McMuffin-makers for nonexistent or minimum-wage jobs. To accept these ineffective palliatives as cellophane-wrapped substitutes for real labor-management reform is to guarantee the realization of the "two-tiered society" so grimly projected by the AFL–CIO's study *The Future of Work* (1985) and to fumble away what may be the last chance of strengthening a more democratic nation for the next century. In broad outline, the necessary reforms are neither radical nor strangers to us. Rather, they point in the direction of a wider diffusion of traditional democratic principles and a greater concern for the individual in the American workplace. Several suggestions for change are especially relevant.

First, there is a need to bolster the due process provisions of employment contracts in order to establish a firm legal foundation of employment and to extend these protections to layoffs. The rationale for this reform is clearly provided by the continuing judicial erosion of the doctrine of "employment at will," the Japanese experience with "lifelong employment," and the desire of American workers expressed in numerous studies for greater security of employment—to say nothing of corporate responsibility to the larger community. This greater commitment to employees would have the laudable side effect of encouraging companies to involve themselves in the kind of long- and intermediate-range planning necessary for their own survival.

Second, most collective bargaining statutes, both state and federal, insist on the exclusion of managerial and supervisory personnel from employee bargaining units. This exclusion is based on the "natural enemies theory" of 1930s industrial labor-management relations. The elimination of these barriers by mutual agreement would encourage a restructuring of the classical worker-boss relationship along lines that are more cooperative and participative, and less adversarial. This could not be effected by mandate. Such a process would always be subject to the right of both employees and employers to choose the proper form for their contractual and professional relationships.

Finally, we must develop mechanisms that will foster an alignment of interest between company and employee—mechanisms that will not only give employees a sense of ownership in their work but will establish them as "citizens of the workplace." We are fortunate in this country to have had more than three hundred and fifty years of experience in developing the constitutional rights and responsibilities of individuals within self-governing entities. Our familiarity with these processes should ease their transference into the arena of corporate governance. We are also fortunate to have the benefit of nearly twenty years of experience with the amalgamation of academic collective bargaining and faculty-shared governance, for it has amply demonstrated their compatibility. The model of faculty unionism and professional autonomy is one that can be valuable in the most dynamic sectors of our national economy.

BIBLIOGRAPHY

American Federation of Labor-Congress of Industrial Organizations. *The Future of Work.* Washington, D.C.: AFL–CIO, 1985.

Bowen, Howard R., and Schuster, Jack H. *American Professors: A National Resource Imperiled.* New York: Oxford University Press, 1986.

Brown, William R. *Academic Politics.* University: University of Alabama Press, 1982.

The Carnegie Commission on Higher Education. *Governance of Higher Education: Six Priority Problems.* New York: McGraw-Hill, 1973.

Chandler, Margaret K., and Julius, Daniel J. "Governance and Unionized Campuses." *Thought and Action: The NEA Higher Education Journal* 1 (Spring 1985): 17–30.

Clark, Burton. *The Academic Life: Small Worlds, Different Worlds.* Princeton: The Carnegie Foundation for the Advancement of Teaching, 1987.

Committee on the Evolution of Work, AFL–CIO. *The Changing Situation of Workers and Their Unions.* Washington, D.C.: AFL–CIO, 1985.

"Joint Statement on Government of Colleges and Universities" (1966), AAUP. *Policy Documents and Reports.* Washington, D.C.: AAUP, 1984.

Mortimer, K. P., and Richardson, R. C. *Governance in Institutions with Faculty Unions: Six Case Studies.* University Park, Pa.: Center for the Study of Higher Education, 1977.

Perkins, James A., ed. *The University as an Organization.* New York: McGraw-Hill, 1973.

Yankelovich, Daniel. *The World at Work.* New York: Octagon Books, 1985.

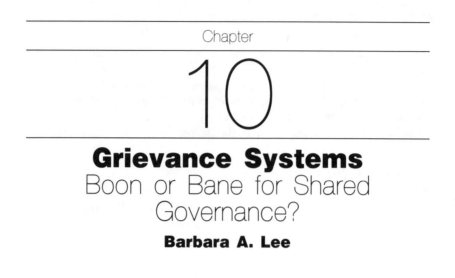

Chapter

10

Grievance Systems
Boon or Bane for Shared Governance?

Barbara A. Lee

The need for systems to review the process by which decisions are
made and the basis for those decisions has been virtually unques-
tioned in higher education; grievance systems exist in both unionized and nonunionized colleges and universities. The literature
about grievance systems, where it exists at all, is descriptive and
generally laudatory. Grievance systems perform the important role
of holding decision-makers (usually, but not always, administrators)
accountable for decisions that affect faculty rights, they provide a
mechanism for addressing procedural violations, and in some institutions they even allow the substance of a decision to be reviewed.

What the literature has not provided, however, is an evaluation
of grievance systems. Have they, in fact, resulted in fairer decisions?
Have they forced decision-makers to be more accountable for their
decisions? Have they provided an effective mechanism for managing
conflict on campus? Have they improved the quality of academic
governance? What *has* been their impact on faculty governance?

This article will discuss the constraints faced by those who use
grievance systems and those who must answer to grievants. It will
describe various advantages and disadvantages of grievance systems
(the "boons" and "banes"), and will conclude by posing some
questions that faculty and administrators might wish to consider
in evaluating the effectiveness of the grievance system on their
campuses.

Scope of Grievance Systems

Before discussing the systems used on campuses to resolve grievances, we must first understand what a grievance is. Estey defines a grievance as a "complaint that a decision that adversely affects an individual in his or her professional or academic capacity has been reached unfairly or improperly."[1] This definition is broad enough to encompass grievances filed either under a collective-bargaining grievance system or one developed on a nonunionized campus, and demonstrates that the term applies to the process by which a decision is made, whatever that decision may be. This means that the complexity of the grievance procedure will be directly related to the complexity of the decision-making process: the more steps (or actors) in the decision-making process, the more complex the review of that decision-making process must be. Therefore, one cannot evaluate a grievance procedure in isolation; it is critical to do so in the context of the way that decisions are made on campus.

Impact on Decision-Making Processes

Grievance procedures tend to formalize and rationalize decision-making and to centralize decision-making power.[2] This rationalization has occurred as use of the grievance process identified policies and practices that were inconsistent, vague, or unfairly applied. While research conducted on unionized campuses has found that the development of grievance systems was among the most significant impacts of collective bargaining, providing a mechanism for reviewing decisions tends to push final decision-making power to the top of the hierarchy and thus enhances administrative power over these decisions.[3] These findings suggest that, although grievance systems may not increase faculty **participation** in decision-making, they do enhance **administrative accountability** for decisions, especially those involving employment matters (promotion, tenure, renewal, merit pay). Although less research has been conducted on grievance systems at nonunionized campuses, Estey's study of grievance procedures at the fifty AAU universities suggests that enhanced accountability is also a by-product on those campuses.[4] With enhanced accountability, however, comes increased complexity, as the documentation necessary to defend a challenge to a decision sometimes becomes as important as the decision itself.

Effect of the Legal System on Grievants

The design of grievance procedures is related to institutional characteristics (control, size, mission) and is affected by the past relationships of the parties and the current decision-making system.[5] However, participants on all campuses face similar constraints posed by the legal system. The most significant constraint is the union's duty of fair representation (*Vaca* v. *Sipes*, 386 U.S. 171 (1967)),[6] which, in practical terms, requires the union to pursue virtually all grievances that have arguable merit. Furthermore, courts generally require bargaining-unit members covered by a contractual grievance procedure to exhaust their internal remedies before litigating in court (with the exception of discrimination cases under the *Alexander* v. *Gardner-Denver* rule), and then tend to defer to the decision of the arbitrator in cases in which the arbitrator's decision binds both parties. While these policies are designed to protect the integrity of the parties' contractually developed dispute resolution mechanisms, they increase the significance of the grievance process because it is often the grievant's sole remedy, and encourage still more complexity and delay in the process.

Grievance Procedures—the Boons and Banes

The Boons

Researchers and faculty leaders agree that grievance systems have generally produced decisions that are fairer, more defensible, and better understood by faculty.[7] Grievance procedures have been useful in identifying policies and practices that permitted inconsistent or biased treatment of faculty, either by their colleagues or by administrators. Grievance procedures have generally enhanced due process on campus by providing faculty members with notice of the performance standards and an opportunity both to learn the rationale for the decision and to challenge the sufficiency of that rationale.

Grievance procedures provide a mechanism for structuring conflict,[8] and administrators and faculty leaders experienced in working under a grievance procedure often prefer a structured approach to resolving problems to one that relies on informal methods or diffuse power. The process also permits the administrators and faculty to share information in a systematic way, and the parties (especially faculty) obtain information they otherwise might not have had access to except, perhaps, by suing the university.

The existence of a grievance procedure that is used frequently to challenge important faculty welfare decisions (promotion, tenure, and so forth) raises the stakes for all decision-makers in the development of clearly articulated, well-documented statements of the reasons for recommendations or decisions.[9] Neither faculty nor administrators generally receive training in how employment decisions should be made, or in the skills of evaluating peers.[10] Forcing each level of the decision process to justify and document its recommendation generally improves the fairness of the decision, and reminds faculty and administrative decision-makers that their responsibilities must be taken seriously and approached professionally.

Finally, a less-formal, but no less important, result of a grievance procedure is that the complaining party is allowed to "blow off steam" and to have one or more bodies listen to his or her complaint. This opportunity may deter litigation, and has been found to be an important tool for effective employment relations in nonacademic organizations[11] as well as in academic ones.[12] Faculty who are not informed how their performance is viewed will assume that it is viewed positively; faculty who are not told the reasons for a denial of promotion, tenure, or a merit increase will assume that the reasons are nonexistent or unsupportable. Permitting faculty to challenge a negative decision within an institution where norms are understood and appreciated, where the reasons for the decision will be explained, and where the sufficiency of the procedures will be examined, not only reduces the tendency of faculty to litigate but protects the university from having its decisions overturned by the courts if litigation ensues.[13] On the other hand, if the grievance procedure unearths biased or discriminatory treatment that the university refuses to rectify, information collected during the grievance process becomes immensely helpful for litigious purposes.

Grievance procedures are a significant component of an effective faculty governance system. The fact that fifty of the most distinguished universities—all nonunionized—have some form of grievance procedure suggests its significance for faculty. But even the most comprehensive grievance system cannot resolve all problems or satisfy all petitioners.

The Banes

In examining the relationship between grievance systems and shared governance, the most significant limitation of a grievance system is the narrowness of its scope. On many unionized campuses, grievances may be filed only about issues covered by the collective-bargaining agreement. Even on campuses where noncontractual issues may be appealed, issues at the heart of the institution's present and future existence—mission, structure, long-range planning, projections of revenue and resource allocation—are usually outside the grievance procedure. Research has demonstrated that faculty unions play little or no part in long-range planning or institutional mission decisions,[14] nor do nonunion faculty governance groups often play a significant role in such decisions. Whether by contract or by custom, the grievance system on most campuses appears to be used primarily by individuals to challenge employment and welfare decisions (promotion, tenure, salary, workload, and the like).

This is not to suggest that the grievance process lends itself well to disputes about resource allocation or institutional mission, or even that adversary processes should be used to challenge such decisions. Resource allocation and organizational planning are management prerogatives in nonacademic settings, and employees do not have the right to bargain over such issues, although they may be invited to participate in them.[15] In academic settings, however, faculty have a history of participation in decisions that could be characterized as "management prerogatives."[16] In fact, the Supreme Court's decision in NLRB v. Yeshiva University (1980) was based upon its perception that the faculty performed significant managerial functions. One of the interesting anomalies of the Yeshiva case and its progeny is the fact that a faculty role in resource allocation decisions or long-range planning is not necessary in order for the faculty to be viewed as "managerial" and thus unable to bargain.[17] And because faculty generally have no formal mechanism for challenging administrative decisions about resource allocation or the institution's future (except, perhaps, for a vote of "no confidence" in one or more administrators), they may focus their energies in a direction where the system may be more responsive to their concerns—faculty welfare issues.

The preoccupation of faculty with their own welfare, and the use of the complex grievance machinery to redress wrongs in this context, consumes an enormous amount of faculty and administrative energy. On some campuses a grievance may be pursued through several levels within an academic unit (such as a college), and then may pass through several administrative layers before it is finally resolved. At an institution with which I am familiar, grievances filed to challenge a negative tenure or promotion decision require an entire academic year of meetings, deliberations, and written reports; filing such a grievance nearly always results in an additional year of employment for a faculty grievant. The complexity of the system and the delays it causes or permits consume a finite resource—faculty and administrative time—that is now unavailable for other matters, such as planning for the institution's future, developing or supporting faculty scholarship and teaching talent, or addressing questions of institutional mission and structure. The pressures on unions to pursue faculty grievances and the interest of faculty committees in giving careful consideration to each challenge are understandable and even laudable, but we must understand the consequences of how our time is spent and to what end. Myron Lieberman has criticized the faculty for making its own welfare the "dominant consideration" and has concluded that "faculty self-government is a major policy disaster."[18] While Lieberman's view may be called an extreme one, an analysis of how faculty spend their governance time and on what kinds of issues tends to support Lieberman's criticism.

Another problem that weakens grievance systems on many campuses is their inability to deal with unfair or biased decisions by a grievant's departmental colleagues. On some unionized campuses, grievances can be filed only against individuals who are not in the faculty bargaining unit. In a survey of lawsuits filed in federal court by faculty claiming that a denial of tenure was discriminatory, the recommendation to deny tenure had, in most instances, come from the plaintiff's departmental colleagues and had merely been affirmed by the administration.[19] Furthermore, most grievance procedures do not permit review of the substance of a decision but only of the procedures used to reach that decision.[20] This results in a grievance system that may hold administrators accountable for decisions but not hold a faculty member's peers accountable for a recommendation that, in fact, becomes the effective decision, for administrators on most college campuses are reluctant to overturn a peer recommendation against promotion or tenure.

The decision to limit grievance procedures to reviewing procedural violations rather than the substantive basis for decisions is founded on a reluctance to permit a reviewing committee to substitute its judgment for the evaluation of a candidate's disciplinary peers concerning that person's scholarship, teaching, or service. This concern is particularly strong in situations in which the grievance procedure culminates in binding arbitration. While a few institutions' collective-bargaining contracts permit a grievant to challenge the substance of a decision, most do not, on the theory that it is inappropriate for an "outside" arbitrator to second-guess the accuracy of an assessment of a faculty member's competence in a discipline with which the arbitrator is probably unfamiliar. This turns the grievant's attention to procedural compliance, and forces the grievant to scour the record for some evidence of a missed deadline, a missing or additional form, or some other error, whether deliberate or innocent. Even if the grievant has convincing evidence that a decision was unfair or biased, if the challenge cannot be linked to a procedural violation, the grievant may not be able to prevail. On the other hand, in decisions in which the substantive basis for a decision is well documented and appropriately considered but a minor procedural violation was committed, the grievant may "win" the grievance and force the entire decision to be repeated. Wasting faculty and administrative time on procedural nitpicking while other governance matters go unaddressed is an unintended but all-too-frequent outcome of academic grievance systems.

In light of these criticisms of grievance systems, what is their implication for decision-making? Is their effectiveness overshadowed by their weaknesses? How can we make them a more effective tool for ensuring accountability and integrity in academic decisions?

Evaluating the Grievance Procedure

Although some of the benefits and problems associated with academic grievance systems are generalizable, the most significant question that each of us must address is the effectiveness of the grievance system on our own campus. While we may be able to borrow ideas from others and learn from their successes and failures, in the end the grievance system we develop must grow out of our institution's mission, norms, and ways of operating. It is constrained by the decision-making system to which it must respond, and it will be affected by the ways in which it is used by faculty and treated by administrators.

We need to ask ourselves some questions about our grievance systems. Does my institution's system take pressure off the governance structure by channeling individual faculty welfare concerns through a well-oiled and reasonably efficient process, or does it drain away energy from governance? If it is the latter, how effective is the faculty voice in significant institutional matters? Who is making the decisions that will determine the nature of this institution in the year 2000?

What proportion of faculty welfare decisions are appealed? If it is substantial, does this suggest that whatever screening mechanism exists (either a union individual or group or some faculty committee on nonunionized campuses) is ineffective? How do we decide what grievances merit the time and energy to pursue? Under what circumstances will we tell disappointed faculty that the decision they wish to challenge does not merit the resources such a challenge will consume?

What is the success rate of grievances? Do all procedural violations result in a remand, or are *de minimis* violations viewed as unworthy of forcing the decision to be repeated? Does the grievance procedure, in effect, guarantee an additional year of employment for faculty denied tenure?

Has the grievance procedure effectively identified weaknesses in the institution's decision-making practices? Have these weaknesses been resolved? Has the grievance procedure forced both faculty and administrators to be more accountable for their recommendations or decisions?

Has the **quality** of decision-making on campus improved as a result of the grievance procedure? Do faculty leaders and academic administrators feel reasonably certain that the process encourages appropriate attention to rigor in faculty welfare decisions while discouraging unfairness? Do candidates for promotion or tenure believe that the system is rigged, or are they reasonably confident that the process will result in a fair decision, even if they may not agree with the outcome?

It is important to remember that grievance systems are tools to resolve conflict and to increase the accountability of academic decision-makers. They cannot be effective if their purpose is misdirected or if they are permitted to function as a routine additional layer in the decision-making process. While faculty may "be" the university, the grievance system should not "be" faculty governance, but one of many ways in which faculty participate in shaping and improving their institutions.

NOTES

1. Martin Estey, "Faculty Grievance Procedures Outside Collective Bargaining: The Experience at AAU Campuses," *Academe* 72 (3) (1986): 8.

2. James P. Begin, "Grievance Mechanisms and Faculty Collegiality: The Rutgers Case," *Industrial and Labor Relations Review* 31 (1978): 295–309.

3. Barbara A. Lee, "Governance at Unionized Four-Year Colleges: Effect on Decision-Making Structures," *Journal of Higher Education* 50 (1979): 565–85.

4. Estey, "Faculty Grievance Procedures Outside Collective Bargaining."

5. Aaron R. Pulhamus, "A Study of the Relationship Between Components of Negotiated Faculty Grievance Procedures and Selected Institutional Factors," unpublished doctoral dissertation, Rutgers University, 1985.

6. Jean McKelvey, ed., *The Changing Law of Fair Representation* (Ithaca, N.Y.: ILR Press, Cornell University, 1985).

7. James P. Begin, "Grievance Mechanisms and Faculty Collegiality: The Rutgers Case," *Industrial and Labor Relations Review* 31 (1978): 295–309; Barbara A. Lee, "Governance at Unionized Four-Year Colleges: Effect on Decision-Making Structures," *Journal of Higher Education* 50 (1979): 565–85; and Karen E. Lindenberg, "The Grievance Process in a Collective Bargaining Setting," *Academe* 72 (3) (1986): 20–24.

8. David W. Leslie and Ronald P. Satryb, "Writing Grievance Procedures on the Basis of Principle," in *Handbook of Faculty Bargaining*, ed. George W. Angell and Edward P. Kelley, Jr. (San Francisco: Jossey-Bass, 1977), pp. 188–217.

9. James P. Begin, "Faculty Bargaining and Faculty Reward Systems," in *Academic Rewards in Higher Education*, ed. Darrell R. Lewis and William E. Becker, Jr., (Cambridge, Mass.: Ballinger, 1979), pp. 246–96.

10. George R. LaNoue and Barbara A. Lee, *Academics in Court: The Consequences of Faculty Discrimination Litigation* (Ann Arbor: University of Michigan Press, 1987).

11. Sumner H. Slichter, James J. Healy, and E. Robert Livernash, *The Impact of Collective Bargaining on Management* (Washington, D.C.: The Brookings Institutions, 1960).

12. LaNoue and Lee, *Academics in Court.*

13. Barbara A. Lee, "Federal Court Involvement in Academic Personnel Decisions: Impact on Peer Review," *Journal of Higher Education* 56 (1985): 38–54.

14. Barbara A. Lee, "Contractually-Protected Governance Systems at Unionized Colleges," *Review of Higher Education* 5 (1982): 69–85.

15. William Ouchi, *Theory Z* (Reading, Mass.: Addison-Wesley, 1981), and Edward E. Lawler, *High-Involvement Management* (San Francisco: Jossey-Bass, 1986).

16. John D. Millett, *The Academic Community* (New York: McGraw-Hill, 1962), and Kenneth P. Mortimer, and T. R. McConnell, *Sharing Authority Effectively* (San Francisco: Jossey-Bass, 1978).

17. Barbara A. Lee and James P. Begin, "Criteria for Evaluating the Managerial Status of College Faculty: Applications of *Yeshiva University* by the NLRB," *Journal of College and University Law* 10 (1983–84): 515–39; and *NLRB* v. *Yeshiva University*, 444 U.S. 672 (1980).

18. Myron Lieberman, "Faculty Self-Government: The Triumph of the Academic Mystique," *Government Union Review* 6 (2) (1985): 40–54.

19. LaNoue and Lee, *Academics in Court.*

20. Estey, "Faculty Grievance Procedures Outside Collective Bargaining."

Part

V

The Political Environment of Campus Governance

Many authors of previous chapters have suggested the growth in importance of external actors as constraints on colleges and universities in recent years. The chapters that follow turn their attention to this changing social and political context for American institutions of higher education in the effort to suggest what these trends may mean for governance. All seem to assume an inherent tension between town and gown as an underlying fact of their analysis. All clearly assume that our colleges and universities must respond to the needs and values of the society they serve. All are agreed that more—or at least different—agencies beyond the campus are looking over the shoulders of colleges and universities today than ever before, and in ways that are bound to affect autonomy and shared governnace. Their opinions differ, however, as to the extent to which these developments should cause alarm within faculties, celebration within the larger community, or the reverse.

Robert Berdahl provides, in Chapter 11, a systematic evaluation of the relations between the campus and a series of groups external to it. Included in his analysis are agents— such as alumni, donors, and collective-bargaining units— that may ordinarily be regarded as subsumed within the internal setting, but which Berdahl argues possess interests that are not always congruent with those whose chief commitment is to the educational mission of the institution as seen from within. His list of external constraints on the campus is a formidable one. His conclusion echoes those of a number of other contributors in arguing the need for a redefinition of the very content of what it is that governance is meant to share.

In Chapter 12, Chester E. Finn, Jr., who was an assistant secretary of education in the Reagan administration, places the blame for increased oversight of higher education by forces beyond the campus squarely on the shoulders of our institutions of higher learning themselves. He argues that lags in faculty productivity, declining educational quality, the ever-increasing costs of higher education, and a growing disjunction between the values promoted in academia and those presumably held throughout the rest of society all have combined to increase public pressure on our institutions of higher learning. Finn's is probably the dissenting voice among the contributors to this volume in his view that "if higher education, left to govern itself, develops as many flaws and eccentricities as the public now perceives, perhaps its autonomy *should* be curbed."

Finally, Chapter 13 presents an assessment of these issues from one of the nation's most noted participants on the American higher educational scene in recent decades. Ernest L. Boyer argues that the federal government has not intervened unduly in the lives of our nation's colleges and universities, but he notes that the era of scarce resources for education through which we have passed (and perhaps still are passing?) has induced on the one hand a kind of hunkering down by campus groups, which have tended to engage in turf warfare as governmental largesse has been cut off, and, on the other side, the "appalling" and contradictory tendency of certain governmental agencies to assume that *more* control of campuses should follow cutbacks in funds to them. One result, according to Boyer, has been a growth in distrust between campus and noncampus agents responsible for the life of higher education in the United States.

As the nation's social and political milieu evolves and changes, so do the demands upon the governance systems of our campuses. The chapters in this concluding section suggest several possible directions in which recent permutations in that evolutionary process may lead us.

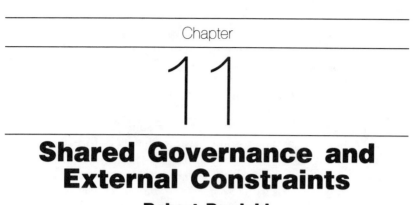

Chapter

11

Shared Governance and External Constraints

Robert Berdahl

The topic of shared governance and external constraints will probably produce some terrain already familiar to many, but I was told long ago in graduate days at Berkeley that people sometimes require more to be reminded than informed. So if I can bring together into a coherent context some things the reader may know in bits and pieces and apply them to the issue of shared governance, perhaps a contribution will have been made.

For example, if, in the discussion of shared governance, one asks what are the relative shares for the faculty, students, trustees, and administrators, this raises the obvious issue of what substantive domain is to be shared. Clearly, if the university or college has fewer powers of self-governance than it used to have, then the debate about these respective roles should reflect that reduced terrain and be realistic rather than purely theoretical.

If external donors or the courts or state governments or federal bureaucratic offices now have the power of control, not even to mention the murky terrain of influence, then the internal debate about respective roles of shared governance should recognize that fact. I use the word "recognize" rather than "accept," because to understand that the domain of autonomy is somewhat reduced from its earlier, broader scale does not mean that one has to accept the legitimacy of the reduction. Rather, as I will later argue, these matters need to be examined almost individually, with balanced judgments made as to whether a particular movement of power from campus to external sources is legitimate from the standpoint of the public interest and not only because the academy would resist it in order to keep maximum control. Those are very tough and difficult judgments to make, and I shall conclude by suggesting that there is a monitoring role for all parties in shared governance and that monitoring cannot be left only to the senior administration and the board of trustees.

It is typically professorial to pause for some definitions, but it should be helpful to clarify some basic concepts before I consider how specific pieces of autonomy have gone here and there. For example, I find it fortuitous that three different studies—the Carnegie Commission's study (1973), *Governance of Higher Education;*[1] a book I wrote for the American Council on Education in 1971, *Statewide Coordination of Higher Education;*[2] and a book by Frank Newman published in 1987, *Choosing Quality: Reducing Conflict Between the State and the University*[3]—all have used some parallel terms. While they do not overlap completely, the parallels are close enough and interesting enough to suggest a common framework. The three of us—Carnegie, Newman, and Berdahl, if you will—talk about something that I called academic freedom, that the Carnegie Commission called intellectual independence, and that Newman discusses in the area of so-called ideological intrusions. All refer to the areas of political, social, and religious orthodoxy and the need to prevent some external agent (in the earlier days, as Walter Metzger has pointed out, it could be the board of trustees itself, but more recently it might be a state legislator or a wealthy donor) from finding that some faculty member has offended an element of orthodoxy, thereby creating tensions between the academy and society.

A second layer is the area of autonomy, and in my 1971 study I broke it down between "procedural autonomy" and "substantive autonomy." The Carnegie Commission used the words "academic independence" for the substantive side and "administrative independence" for the procedural side. Frank Newman has put in parallel terms of "political intrusions" for the substantive side and "bureaucratic intrusions" for the procedural side.

I will not dwell any further on these definitional matters, but I will use, for want of better terms, my own vocabulary of academic freedom and procedural and substantive autonomy to look at relations between the university and external societies.

For many years I have been greatly stimulated by a fine essay by Walter Metzger. In fact, a former colleague at Buffalo and I liked it so much that we put it into a book of readings called

Higher Education in American Society.[4] The Metzger essay is "Academic Freedom in De-localized Academic Institutions." In it, he contrasts the relatively simpler environment of the typical college in 1915, at the time that the American Association of University Professors (AAUP) emerged and gave us its definition of academic freedom with the highly complex and interdependent world of current academic institutions.

In 1915 a so-called localized college had fairly distinct physical boundaries with the adjoining town, ruled more or less in loco parentis over its relatively small student body drawn from, perhaps, 2 percent of the college-age cohort, and exercised quite arbitrary powers over those students. It had a relatively straightforward curriculum taught by a faculty whose primary responsibility was teaching, with perhaps incidental research. It made relatively few demands on society in terms of either appropriations or other needs, and gave relatively modest direct service to society, not being heavily involved in gross national product or defense efforts. As a consequence, it had considerable autonomy. Although one does not want to look back with glowing eyes to a rosy period that never was, compared to today the powers of self-governance were certainly greater then. Since the college was not part of a multi-campus system, it usually had a local board of trustees. There were few intruding statewide boards; the federal government played no particular role at all; and there were few, if any, faculty unions.

Therefore, as Metzger's essay points out, the issues of academic freedom or autonomy were very different from those we now confront. In fact, he says,

One of the most important of the transformations has been the flow of decisional power from authorities on the campus to those resident outside. Richer, larger, more complex than ever before, the typical modern institution of higher learning is less self-directive than ever before. It has become, to coin a word, de-localized, with the consequences we are just beginning to perceive. De-localization has not been a single process, but a congeries of processes all working in the same direction and achieving a common end. The engulfing of many universities by the central city with the result that everything they do in the way of land use becomes imbued with political implications and ensnarled in municipal law. . . . The growth of bureaucratized philanthropy is a principal source of academic innovation. The subordination of judgment of admissions officers, the legislative judgments concerning civil rights, the involvement of universities in social welfare, and, thus, with clients it can serve but not control, may be considered other forces. So, too, the integration of public higher education[5] the assault by the courts on the principle of extraterritoriality and the enlargement of federal influence due to federal sponsorship of research and, of course, access for students in affirmative action.

Metzger's final point in his essay was that academe had been overly focused on traditional notions of academic freedom, and that, as a consequence, autonomy issues were neglected.

No process of de-localization unless it threatened the wellbeing of professors was presumed to violate academic freedom and . . . without a violation of academic freedom, no insult to the university seemed to cause broad alarm. The autonomy and the integrity of the university, these heavenly things on earth, are not contained in that philosophy.[6]

So Metzger urged that the 1915 definition be broadened. What his essay did not have time to do was to examine the areas of autonomy, whether procedural or substantive, in their sensitive relationships with all the different external constituencies.

I will try an exercise in what Eric Ashby, in Great Britain, called the "ecology of higher education" by looking at some of the environmental elements and trying to suggest examples of the kinds of problems that emerge. Some are in the area of what we call influence, those legitimate pushes and pulls in a democratic society, in which pluralistic forces operate. A university or college can claim no immunity from those forces and, in fact, that lack of immunity is probably healthier for them. Nevertheless, they require scrutiny and evaluation. In other areas it is mandatory authority that has moved elsewhere, and one must comply unless one is convinced that the move is illegitimate; then one can counterattack either through the courts or the political process.

I start with town and gown and move further out. First come our good friends, the alumni, who, on the one hand, support alma mater with their money, their enthusiasm, and their volunteer efforts. But on occasion, their enthusiasm can go too far, particularly in such areas as intercollegiate athletics, where there have been instances of gross interference with campus decisions and priorities. We have all read relevant headlines in the newspapers. In the *Chronicle of Higher Education* there is a nearly unending series of horror stories about alumni with misplaced zeal trying to get the campus to do things differently than perhaps the academic or administrative participants in shared governance would accept. At Michigan State an open conflict broke out between the alumni association and the university's board, and a power confrontation nearly developed.

As a further example, the president of the University of Kentucky had to deal with Governor John Y. Brown, who, under alumni influence, wanted to help the president choose the next football coach. One could continue down that street with a whole host of anecdotes, but the point is that a university that thinks it can govern itself will learn that the alumni that it has roused to fervor in the support of alma mater may be a mixed blessing. Not only do they give money and support, but sometimes they want to help control the academy's decisions.

The same is true with donors, whether very powerful single individuals or foundations. Father Timothy S. Healy, President of Georgetown University, with some embarrassment, decided a few years after the fact to return to Muammar al Qaddafi and Libya a substantial gift for the establishment of a chair or an institute of Middle Eastern studies when, obviously, Libya was not going to permit any candidates of the Hebrew faith to be seriously considered for appointment. Clearly, that kind of conditional gift would violate some of the basic academic norms about holding open searches for the best-qualified candidates, even for endowed chairs. That kind of limitation could not be accepted with any self-respect and so the gift was ultimately returned—and should probably not have been accepted in the first place, one says with the wisdom of hindsight.

One also thinks of John Silber at Boston University, who was chided for having said, when confronted with criticism about admitting the sons of wealthy Middle Eastern sheikhs to Boston University, that there was a long and honorable historical precedent for the selling of indulgences. So the academy must handle the issue of wealthy donors ready to contribute money if only the academy will move in directions the donors desire. Since it is very hard to turn down money, it must be difficult to make such decisions, but those issues have to be faced.

I have already mentioned foundations. Basically, I think they have had a positive overall impact when they stimulated us to innovation and change in ways that we might not have attempted if left alone. Nevertheless, there is an element of inducing or, if you will, seducing the academy to move in directions that certain foundations feel are priority areas. And so again, in defining autonomy, you must consider the extent to which an academy is pulled off its true course, as defined from inside, by the lure of substantial amounts of money.

Accreditation is, I think, also basically benign; yet, some specialized groups can penetrate far into academe and lay down particular requirements for compliance that reach deep into autonomy. A doctoral student of mine at the University of Maryland wrote her dissertation about the process whereby the University of Baltimore achieved AACSB (American Association of Colleges of Schools of Business) accreditation. There were many detailed requirements about full-time/part-time faculty, and faculty with terminal qualifications were required to teach certain percentages of the total student enrollment (they had to switch faculty from day to night courses, and shift the faculty with terminal degrees into the big sections so that they would cover a larger percentage of students). Many things that academe traditionally thought were a matter of internal governance have clearly been delivered piecemeal to different specialized accrediting groups—business here, social work there, nursing there, dentistry there, library science there, architects there, chemistry there—need I go on? The point is that, little by little, academe has given a finger and a toe until the body has shrunk considerably.

I think the motivation of individual specialized accrediting processes is to improve the quality of higher education, and the demands they make of academe are efforts to improve each particular program. Nevertheless, from the standpoint of governance and determining, as a matter of internal decision-making, the balance among the various programs and the priorities for future growth or retrenchment—an increasingly tough agenda item for governance to confront—those priorities are obviously distorted because some players have external leverage on the academy through these specialized accrediting ultimatums. So again, in our definition of autonomy, we must take that into consideration.

I also look at collective bargaining as another external actor. I know that the membership of the faculty union comes from inside and so "we" are "they", but the center of gravity of the union in the legal sense is external to the academy. Thus even though, like a wealthy foundation or an accreditation visit, the motives of the process may be benign—looked at dispassionately in terms of the governance issue—a faculty union is still external to the academy. In defining autonomy, one must consider the fact that a union might bring into the collective-bargaining agreement certain matters that go far beyond wages, retirement plans, and health benefits, and include teaching loads, faculty/student ratios, and many other things that earlier were considered the heart of academe. I would therefore urge that faculty and staff unions be considered among the potential players in a redefinition of autonomy.

Then there are state governments, the area in which I personally have done the most work. The role of state government has expanded enormously since the 1960s. There are now statewide boards in forty-seven of the fifty states, and even little pretenses of them in the other three. The states create the legal framework within which universities must operate. In the public sector the government either appoints or elects members of the boards of trustees. There is the obvious issue of state appropriations of tax dollars and the coordination and regulation framework in which states are increasingly influencing, if not controlling, institutional role and mission, saying that a given institution should become a certain type of institution and that it does not have the freedom to become anything that it and its trustees aspire for it to be. There is also program approval power that says that, before an institution can establish a new academic program, it must pass through certain layers of approval. There is budget review and, increasingly now in state governments, a domain of accountability called "performance audit," in which state governments are no longer content to have appropriations generated by input analysis.

Input analysis involves questions such as the following: How many students do you expect and how do they translate into full-time-equivalent enrollment? How many new faculty positions does that new full-time-equivalent student count justify? How many new square feet of classroom will you need in the capital plant? Those were input factors that were relatively easier to handle in the old days of formula budgeting; but now in state government there is an increasing desire and even insistence directed not just toward higher education but toward public policy in general, and state governments begin to evaluate the output, the product, the performance. Many states have performance audit staffs, connected either with the state auditor or sometimes with specialized groups called, as in Virginia, the joint legislative audit and review commission. These are no longer green-eyeshade accountants who come in to audit the books for compliance with legality or efficiency. They get into questions of effectiveness that raise normative value considerations. These multidisciplinary teams are drawn from economics, public administration, and social psychology, and include statisticians and accountants; they ask some very tough questions about what the public agency in question is doing. And when they turn to us in the academy, we are not yet very ready to answer "We are producing quality graduates." "How do you know they are quality graduates?" "Well, we know because we are doing it." This answer is not good enough, and I anticipate an increasingly complex agenda between the university and the state government about how good we are at doing what we say we are doing.

Alongside that is a more attractive element of state government that intrudes little on autonomy. This is called incentive funding, in which incentive is placed out front in the form of dollars ("green carrots") for certain categorical programs. For example, the Funds for Excellence program in Virginia is a small fund for the improvement of postsecondary education that does some very interesting things with colleges. The program generates its own proposals to improve the general education scores of students in the first two years, or to make the engineering curriculum better, or to institute writing across the curriculum, or to get computers into the humanities. The projects are quite interesting, and I find that kind of agenda between the academy and state government to be fairly upbeat and in strong contrast to something like mandatory testing, which is imposed from the state down.

Frank Newman's 1987 book, *Choosing Quality*, covers the state government role in considerable detail. He gives little unidentified anecdotes on ideological intrusions, political intrusions, and bureaucratic intrusions, page by page, and it is quite interesting to read what is still going on in all three of those domains. State governments have become less intrusive because of ideological motives, impinging less in the area of academic freedom, and that is good news. But in the two other domains—the bureaucratic or procedural, as I call it, or, as Newman calls it, the substantive political area—there is still plenty to worry about. We want to keep looking at academic freedom, but, in the meantime, all these other agenda items have come up in the area of autonomy (or bureaucratic or procedural controls). We want to monitor them as well, because they affect academe and they certainly affect the debate about shared governance.

In the federal government, one of the three main elements of activity, particularly since World War II, has been to create the research process that Metzger mentioned; there the agenda is not one of any mandatory control, except that institutions have to subject themselves to the requirements of funding agencies if they want a share of their monies. Clark Kerr's book *The Uses of the University*[7] says that the three main impacts of the federal grant university have been to emphasize research over teaching, graduate programs over undergraduate, and science over humanities. To the extent that those three general influences have been pervasive in the flow of federal money, the academy must take that into consideration and decide whether it can go along with those three influences and whether it retains any countervailing forces with which to try to strengthen undergraduate education, humanities, and teaching.

I see those countervailing forces on the horizon. Right now state governments are concentrating on improving the quality of undergraduate education, and they are trying to drag the faculty, kicking and screaming, back into the classroom. There I see the state government as countervailing some of the federal influences, which makes for an interesting set of interplays in our federal-state relations. But the federal research domain has those pervasive influences, and there are also some bureaucratic controls at the federal level. Research universities fought against some of the more incredibly nitpicking requirements of compliance, as in an A95 directive in which the university would have to account for a faculty member's time throughout the whole week in order to know how much of it to charge to a given federal contract, to determine whether that person was spending an hour on teaching or research or public service. It gets ludicrous because, when you read a book, it is for several purposes, and it is kind of silly to overdo that kind of detailed requirement.

There was a committee out of the academy that negotiated with the national government about such regulations and, to give the Reagan administration credit, their deregulation orientation has led them to back off a little and that has been welcome.

Another aspect of federal programs has been to broaden access, and there it has had a basically benign impact on higher education. There are institutions like Grove City and Hillsdale College, which do not want to tangle with the federal government even through student access. In an effort to stay clear of federal jurisdiction, there have been some court cases like the Grove City case and others in which some campuses did not want to allow the federal subsidies to students to bring the campus under federal jurisdiction. Most of us, though, have not had that problem, and we gladly welcome students with Pell grants, with work-study, and with federal loans. Many colleges are probably now dependent on the continuation of those federal programs for their survival.

The third domain of the federal program since World War II has been that of social justice and affirmative action. There, of course, one finds the academy entangled deeply in federal jurisdiction, particularly through the court system. In the *Regents of the University of California* v. *Bakke* case in California, a white student denied admission to the medical school at the University of California–Davis claimed that the quota system for minorities denied him equal protection under the law—a kind of exercise in reverse discrimination. Enormous legal hassles can develop over the admissions process and the hiring of faculty and staff. In 1977 in *Adams* v. *Califano* (430 F. Supp. 118), some courts in the fourteen southern states had made major decisions that affected what campuses could do by way of new programs, the enhancement of the predominantly black colleges, including even consent decrees that students, trustees, and faculty of other races would be brought in. Again, one probably welcomes this as a necessary reaction to academe's own neglect of a moral agenda, but in terms of autonomy and the governing process, you have to realize that those decisions are no longer made only on campus. I said earlier that I was going to speak of things my audience already knew. This is one such thing, but when we add that dimension to all the others I have mentioned, it means that the academy now governs itself far, far less than it used to do.

In loco parentis tended to disappear long ago (and probably well it should have), and the courts have gone far in examining procedural due process. Have students accused of some disciplinary transgression been allowed careful due process inside the academy? The old days of the dean of students arbitrarily suspending or expelling some students have long since gone, and the college student personnel officers now need a good legal counsel to guide them. But normally, on substantive matters, the courts have deferred to academe, just as they have traditionally deferred to the political branches of government. In Missouri a woman named Horowitz was dropped by a medical school in her third year because her clinical work was considered unsatisfactory, although she received A's in most of her courses. She said, "I'm not going to practice medicine. I want my M.D. just to do research." She sued the University of Missouri, claiming they had treated her unfairly because she was getting A's in her nonclinical work. The university had brought in a second group of medical personnel from outside to judge her clinical work, and the second group had also found her wanting. The court's attitude was, "We're not going to touch it. If the medical faculty thinks she's not qualified, we're not going to substitute our judgment for theirs."

In a recent case in California, however, a court determined, if I read *The Washington Post* correctly, that the University of California agricultural extension program and research program had not conformed to the spirit or the letter of the Morrill Land Grant Act of 1862 and the Second Land Grant Act because too much of its research helped agribusiness and not enough helped the small family farmer. Evidently there was some language in the original land grant law (which, to be truthful, I have never read paragraph by paragraph) urging universities to do research on agriculture and help society without distinguishing between small family farmers and agribusiness (which in 1862 probably did not exist). But here we have the court intervening to examine a university's research program and deciding substantively, "It's not the right kind of program." Now, I don't know if that will be appealed. Interestingly enough, if the *Post* can be believed, the U. S. Department of Agriculture sided with the University of California, deciding that it had conformed to the land grant act and that it was a public interest group in California, like Nader's Raiders, that was representing the consumer or the small farm family business that had taken the university to court. If that were to go through, we might find—and I want to be cautiously speculative here—that the courts will not be as reticent as historically they seem to have been in second-guessing the substance of academic judgment. If that were to be true, we would have to reopen the question of relations between the academy and the courts which, until now, had been largely confined to due process issues.

University autonomy, then, is not what it used to be. It was never total, but the bits and pieces lost here and there on the road toward a system of mass access to higher education have been cumulatively substantial. Is the price too high? That is a very subjective judgment that needs an answer. I am willing to say no. I have had the privilege of attending two conferences in 1986 and 1987 with British colleagues on access and quality in higher education, and the generalization, to oversimplify our discussion, was that the British were very good on quality in their universities but were found wanting on access. They themselves said so. They said it was a tragedy in their society that higher education was being confined to such a relatively small proportion of their population, and that many potentially talented young men and women were not being allowed the opportunity to develop their talent. So they felt they had quality and needed access.

We may have achieved more in the area of access, although we still have an unfinished agenda in terms of certain disadvantaged students, but there are a lot of quality problems. Would I surrender some of our access for higher quality? No, I am optimistic enough to think we can have both. Just as the British are trying to expand their quality system of higher education, so I think we can improve the quality of our broadened system. But I would not return to the halcyon days of the localized institution of 1915 even though, in some ways, it looks rather attractive—Mr. Chips in his small academy teaching a few students across a kind of Mark Hopkins log.

We must have a broader system of access. There are numbers of students who present complexity for the curriculum, complexity for the faculty, and cost to the state and the nation, and with this complexity and those costs come issues of accountability that will require the sharing of power, not only on campus through governance but off campus through a very complicated governance system.

We must redefine the shared governance turf. I would urge that, as part of its role in shared governance, the faculty not only look at internal campus matters but appoint a faculty committee that, as a matter of course, monitors the institution's external relations. Its purpose should not be to second-guess every act that the senior administration or board of trustees performs, because they have to be left alone to get on with their business and, as full-time people, will be able to bring more resources to bear than amateur faculty members spending part of their time on a committee. But I would urge that a faculty committee take the commanding heights of policy surveillance and stay in touch with what is going on— for example, monitoring the campus's policy about accepting or rejecting gifts. Is anybody looking at that policy? Is anyone looking at the accreditation process? Is there a proper balance between specialized accrediting and the demands it makes, or does the academy need to stand on its hind legs and say, "Enough! Back off a little!"? On relations with state government, are the particular powers between the academy and the state capital about right, or has the state attempted to go too far and, if so, how does the academy form alliances in society to get the state government to back off? (On occasion this has happened. The State University of New York prompted the federal government to appoint a national blue-ribbon commission to investigate SUNY control by state government. After the commission issued a powerful report, the state backed off somewhat.) So it is not totally unthinkable, although I would have to tell you that achieving a slight reversal in the encroachment of some external constituency on academe does not come easily.

The AAUP, with which I have had some previous association, has a Committee R that deals with state and federal policies; it is important that the faculty also be aware of this dimension of campus autonomy as well as our concern with academic freedom. And the faculty senate, if it is a self-respecting body, ought to have some standing committee that monitors those issues and, on occasion when they are concerned about possible abuse, speaks to the proper administrative or trustee sources.

NOTES

1. Carnegie Commission on Higher Education, *Governance of Higher Education* (New York: McGraw-Hill, 1973).

2. R. O. Berdahl, *Statewide Coordination of Higher Education* (Washington, D.C.: American Council on Education, 1971).

3. F. Newman, *Choosing Quality* (Denver: Education Commission of the States, 1987).

4. P. G. Altbach and R. O. Berdahl, eds., *Higher Education in American Society* (Buffalo, N.Y.: Prometheus Books, 1981).

5. In which Metzger means moving into formal public systems, with authority strongly moved off campus.

6. Walter Metzger, "Academic Freedom in De-localized Academic Institutions," in Altbach and Berdahl, *Higher Education in American Society*, p. 63.

7. C. Kerr, *Uses of the University* (Cambridge, Mass.: Harvard University Press, 1982).

Chapter

12

Context for Governance
Public Dissatisfaction and Campus Accountability
Chester E. Finn, Jr.

In the 1980s, recognition of education as a matter critical to U.S. economic and political vitality has heightened public concern about all levels of schooling, including postsecondary. For years, our colleges and universities were hailed as the crowning achievement of American education. Even today, some campus faculty and administrators would have us believe that the glory of higher education has never been greater. After all, the industry is coming off a remarkable surge of growth—a 62-percent increase in the number of institutions since the late 1950s, a concomitant increase of nearly three-and-a-half times in the number of students enrolled. With some 25 percent of adults in the U.S. work force possessing a college degree, our colleges and universities are serving a larger proportion of the American people than ever before.

But there is another side to the story, less worthy of celebration. Rising tuition, declining productivity, dubious practices, and slipshod quality have grown so pervasive in academe that public pressure is mounting for government officials to take some sort of action. If higher education, left to govern itself, develops as many flaws and eccentricities as the public now perceives, perhaps its autonomy *should* be curbed. That is a simple statement of a complex matter, but it is broadly descriptive of the mind-set of today's restive public.

Academics want no constraints on their freedom, of course; nor do many state or federal officials yearn to intervene in campus affairs. Most would prefer to leave collegiate governance in the hands of campus administrators and faculty. Public officials do have a responsibility, however, to make sure that the public interest is well served and the public's dollars wisely invested. The taxpayer pays over two-thirds of the bill for higher education in this country, and it is within the citizen's rights to expect that these generously subsidized colleges and universities will provide a quality education broadly compatible with the values and principles of a democratic society—and will do so with reasonable efficiency and at reasonable cost.

These are the four ends and outcomes that I judge the public wants: educational quality, institutional efficiency, reinforcement of fundamental societal values, and a fair price tag. When there is evidence that all four are being achieved, most people will cheerfully agree that the campuses ought to be sovereign with respect to their internal affairs. But when there is evidence to the contrary, the specter of state involvement arises. Today that specter is real. The cherished values of campus autonomy and self-governance are threatened by four conditions roughly parallel to the quartet of desiderata just set forth.

First, the price of attending college has skyrocketed. With tuition in the 1980s climbing at a rate two-and-a-half times faster than the cost of living, the sticker price is fast growing beyond the reach of what most Americans believe they will be able to afford in coming years. In 1988–89 it cost $20,000 to attend some of the nation's best-known private colleges. The $100,000 bachelor's degree looms on the horizon.

The price has risen, we know, largely because campus expenditures are rising. In 1986–87, colleges and universities, after adjusting for inflation, spent 24 percent more per full-time equivalent student than in 1981–82. But these spending hikes have not all resulted from inexorable forces beyond the control of campus administrators. Howard Bowen has sagely noted that colleges tend to maximize revenues and then spend everything they take in,[1] an impulse that often leads to needless outlays and self-indulgent consumption.

In a 1988 profile of Mount Holyoke College, Barry Werth recounts how that institution's leadership deliberately departed from its "elegant frugality" of the past to become, well, simply elegant.[2] The college spent $100,000 redecorating the president's house and nearly $2 million on a new "equestrian facility" as part of an overall effort to gussy up the campus. This approach, which one Holyoke dean termed the "Chivas Regal" strategy, is not limited to western Massachusetts; the sticker price has become part of many a college's image. "People do judge quality by price," admitted Kalamazoo College president David Breneman during a seminar on college finance. "Right or wrong, price is a message to the public of what we are. I do nothing for my college if I am a good citizen and I raise tuition only five percent." (Kalamazoo's 1988–89 price tag, 9 percent greater than the previous year's, rose at about the average rate for four-year private institutions.)

Second, colleges and universities display declining productivity. At a time when society expects virtually all its major enterprises to boost their per-unit outputs or lower their unit costs, those within the ivied walls somehow deem themselves immune. Maybe there is a college somewhere that is already putting its personnel and resources to optimal use, but I've never encountered it. Far more common are campuses where the average faculty member teaches fewer hours and fewer students than a decade ago; where even the heaviest teaching loads rarely involve more than about twenty-three hours of "teaching-connected activities (including office and other student content hours)" per week[3]; where the academic calendar is weeks shorter than it once was; where expensive physical plants sit idle and libraries empty four to six months of the year; and where a growing share of college revenue is swallowed by administrative overhead (a budget item that is growing at more than twice the rate of instructional expenditures).

Third, too many universities are losing the spirit of open inquiry and have made themselves inhospitable to views different from the prevailing political attitudes on campus. This violates both the fundamental American norms of fair play and free expression and the academy's vaunted traditions of open inquiry and the unfettered search for truth.

Several recent events point to growing intellectual intolerance and closed-mindedness in academe. In 1987–88 the faculty at Colby College blocked students from meeting with Central Intelligence Agency recruiters; the University of Massachusetts' Afro-American studies department ousted a member for criticizing black novelist James Baldwin. At Harvard, despite exhortations from both the liberal and conservative student newspapers that administrators take a stronger stand against the kind of protests that disrupted and nearly prevented Nicaraguan Contra leader Alfredo Cesar from speaking there, the faculty dean stands firm on the school's policy of relying "on basic human decency as the ultimate corrective mechanism to ensure freedom of speech."[4]

Stanford, where 80 percent of the faculty are Democrats, flexed its mandatory retirement rule in 1988 to force the resignation of sixty-five-year-old W. Glenn Campbell, director of the generally conservative Hoover Institution, a prominent campus research center. Yet Stanford trustees hired back their sixty-four-year-old former president for a five-year term as director of the university's new International Institute. Such double standards and partisan maneuvering fly in the face of the liberal ideals that ought to be upheld on every campus. If institutions devoted to learning and ideas close their doors to free inquiry and divergent opinions, how can they transmit these dispositions to students? If students do not acquire a predilection for free speech and reasoned debate while on campus, through what means will that disposition be preserved in our society at large?

Fourth, the baccalaureate degree is no longer a reliable guarantee of even basic literacy. To be sure, higher education suffers from skimpy information on student learning outcomes. But the available evidence *is* discouraging. In 1985, for example, the National Assessment of Educational Progress (NAEP) examined literacy levels among twenty-one to twenty-five-year-olds and found that roughly half of the young adults *who had graduated from college* could not perform such fundamental intellectual tasks as summarizing a newspaper column, calculating a 10-percent tip for lunch, or making sense of a bus schedule.

It may be noted that reading bus schedules and figuring dinner tips are not skills that most colleges set out to teach. On the other hand, colleges *do* require students to perform a good bit of reading, thinking, and writing—or so we assume—and these intellectual activities surely ought to yield graduates who can perform tasks that it is reasonable to expect *high-school* graduates to be able to do.

To be sure, the NAEP study found young adults who had not been to college even worse off. And because these abilities *should* have been acquired in high school, it can be argued, the elementary-secondary system is largely to blame for these deficits. That is at least partly true. But college entrance standards powerfully influence the exit standards of the elementary/secondary system. And when most of higher education embraced the policy of open admission, the effect on the schools was grave. Higher education in effect signaled that youngsters need not strain themselves preparing for college because they would get in no matter how well or ill prepared they were.

So now most colleges and universities—except for the handful of famously selective institutions—face hordes of poorly prepared students. Two out of five freshmen show up on Florida's and Georgia's public campuses needing remedial instruction, as do nearly half the entering freshmen under twenty-one years of age in Tennessee. In New Jersey, not even one in three of the entering freshmen is proficient in computation or verbal skills; just 15 percent can solve elementary algebra problems. What is happening in these and other states indicates that remedial instruction has mushroomed on campuses across the country, soaking up resources and energies that should be spent on bona-fide college-level teaching and learning.

Inadequately prepared students are by no means the only symbol of declining academic quality. The college curriculum, once a reasonably coherent intellectual framework, has decayed into a grab bag of courses governed, if at all, by distribution requirements. Practically nowhere is there a real "core" to the curriculum. Several years ago, the Association of American Colleges complained that "as for what passes for a college curriculum, almost anything goes. We have reached a point at which we are more confident about the length of a college education than its content and purpose."[5]

On many campuses, the faculty has backed off from any collective effort to identify the skills, knowledge, and dispositions that ought to be the hallmarks of an education at their institution. It is so hard, after all, to forge consensus on these weighty matters; it is so much easier to let the students do the deciding. As Syracuse professor Ralph Ketcham explains, faculty have "simply quit arguing about what students should study. . . . They [have] said to students, 'Take whatever you want.' And then many teachers, too, decided to teach just what they wanted, the favorite part of their subject. Chaos might be a good word to describe the result."[6]

Recent statements by other faculty indicate the unlikelihood that this situation will soon change. Rutgers Vice Provost Catharine R. Stimpson opined in 1988 that creating a core curriculum is impossible and, if it were not impossible, it would be undesirable anyway, for it would exclude "popularizers and pleasure givers," such as Krazy Kat cartoons.[7] A professor of literature at the University of Pennsylvania recently declaimed that choosing between Virginia Woolf and Pearl Buck is "no different from choosing between a hoagy and a pizza. . . . I'm one whose career is dedicated to the day when we have a disappearance of those standards."[8]

Such comments inspire little public confidence in the judgment and reliability of college faculty. And the 1980s have indeed witnessed mounting dissatisfaction with the fruits of faculty labors. In 1986 the nation's governors reported that today's college graduates are "not as well educated as students of past decades. Gaps between ideal academic standards and actual student learning are widening."[9] Early in 1988 a Cornell poll revealed that most national opinion leaders believe a "major problem with higher education today is that students are not learning the basic skills."[10]

Similar criticisms have arisen from some quarters within academe. Glenn Dumke, chancellor emeritus of the California state university system, comments that "Today, a bachelor's degree holder might very well be unable to write and spell effectively, be awkward in oral expression, have little or no knowledge of history or the American business system and have no competence in math beyond simple arithmetic or basic algebra."[11]

The fact that Allan Bloom's book *The Closing of the American Mind* was on best-seller lists for over a year is one indication that concern about higher education is spreading.[12] A crisis of public confidence in the academy is festering, and it will not be arrested without potent medicine. Colleges and universities have got to slow the pace of rising tuition and cut unnecessary costs. Campus leaders need to pare back their budgets. Faculty and administrators should find ways to increase institutional productivity, perhaps by increasing instructional work loads, consolidating low-enrollment programs, eliminating nonessential courses, promoting summer study and off-season facility use, improving intercampus facility sharing, and adding days to the semester. They surely must guarantee that their campuses are places where free speech flourishes, where unpopular ideas receive a fair hearing, where reasoned criticism and healthy debate reign, and where faculty personnel policies are shielded from ideology and partisan views.

Finally, faculty and campus administrators must make a concerted effort to restore integrity to the college degree. That will not happen—at least, no one can rest confident it will happen—if a condition noted by the nation's governors several years ago continues, namely the condition that "learning . . . is *assumed* to take place as long as students take courses, accumulate hours, and progress 'satisfactorily' toward a degree."[13] Rather, as the Study Group on the Conditions of Excellence in American Higher Education concluded in 1984, colleges and universities must "produce *demonstrable improvements* in student knowledge, capacities, skills, and attitudes between entrance and graduation" if they are to move toward education excellence.[14]

Some faculty oppose the idea of assessing student skills and knowledge, claiming that the learning we cherish most is least susceptible to measurement. There is a morsel of truth here, but there is also a bit of a cop-out. The state of assessment is not perfect but, in the words of the Association of American Colleges, it "is a feasible art."[15] And assessment delivers clear benefits. Those campuses where comprehensive systems for measuring student learning and outcomes are now in place report improvements in curricula, instruction, collegiality, student advisement, retention, placement rates, and certification exam scores.[16] Most important, at these institutions, writes higher-education-assessment expert Peter Ewell, "it appears that students are in fact learning more."[17] Solid student learning outcomes are what the public wants and what colleges and universities must become accountable for. If campuses fail to furnish evidence of student learning, they invite government intrusion.

At the federal level, we in the U.S. Department of Education have sought to promote assessment and accountability through new regulations that encourage the nation's eighty-odd voluntary accrediting agencies to focus more systematically on student outcomes, to examine such criteria as test results, licensing exams, graduate and professional school admissions, and job placement rates. Also, through the department's Fund for the Improvement of Postsecondary Education, we are supporting more than two dozen projects that seek to develop indicators, instruments, mechanisms, and systems for assessing student achievement and outcomes in higher education.

State officials realize that jobs and economic development in their jurisdictions are inextricably linked to the quality of their colleges and universities, and many recognize assessment as an indispensable tool for fostering—and monitoring—such quality. Most states have begun to talk about assessing student learning and outcomes in higher education. According to a 1988 National Governors' Association survey, 20 states have already acted to develop or implement policies on assessment; 12 states are discussing the possibility of adopting such policies; and 4 states now have assessment programs in place.[18]

It is in the interest of states, the nation, and individual institutions to install feedback mechanisms by which information on student learning (and other kinds of outcomes) can be collected, analyzed, and used to guide institutional decisions. In the opinion of the Association of American Colleges, the "process [of assessment] can be a low-cost, high-yield activity"[19]—no small claim, considering that higher education in the United States is a $124-billion industry absorbing some 2.7 percent of the gross national product and involving about 6 percent of the population as employees and students. It comes as no surprise, then, that many major higher education associations have endorsed the assessment movement and that states are beginning to demand evidence of student learning. What is disturbing is that so few institutions have implemented these recommendations.

This is why, as the National Governors' Association asserts, "it is essential that states maintain the pressure to assess despite the many vocal arguments against it."[20] As Frank Newman concluded in his 1987 study of major state universities, these institutions (and I believe his comment pertains to most colleges as well), if left totally to themselves, "will evolve toward self-interest rather than public interest."[21] Clearly, policy makers must act to prevent that from happening.

Public pressure is mounting for costs and prices to be brought under control, for freedom of inquiry to be guaranteed, for institutional productivity and student learning to be improved. Campus leaders who commit themselves to these goals and then show actual progress in achieving them will give their institutions a decided advantage. They will also go far toward vouchsafing their own continued sovereignty. Most public officials would prefer that colleges and universities see to these matter themselves, for self-governance and institutional diversity are virtues of American higher education that few policymakers would forfeit by gratuitously meddling in campus processes. But the public and its elected officials must see evidence of results.

The current challenge affords a window of opportunity. Institutions that act with reasonable speed and determination can chart their own course of accountability. Those that continue to tarry

may in time find someone else doing it for them. This choice—
and today it is just that—will powerfully influence the degree to
which campus sovereignty endures in American higher education.

NOTES

1. Howard R. Bowen, *The Costs of Higher Education* (San Francisco: Jossey-Bass, 1980).

2. Barry Werth, "Why Is College So Expensive?", This article first appeared in *New England Monthly* (January 1988): 39, and was reprinted in *Change: The Magazine of Higher Learning*, XX, 2 (March/April 1988), pp. 13–15.

3. Robert Boice, "Is Released Time an Effective Component of Faculty Development Programs?", *Research in Higher Education* 26, no. 3 (1987): 318.

4. Thomas Sowell, "Campus Storm Troopers," *The Washington Times*, Feb. 2, 1988.

5. *Integrity in the College Curriculum: A Report to the Academic Community* (Washington: Association of American Colleges, 1985), p. 2.

6. *Richmond Times-Dispatch*, Sept. 6, 1987.

7. Catharine R. Stimpson, "Is There a Core in This Curriculum? And Is It Really Necessary?", *Change* 20, 2 (March/April 1988): 28.

8. Joseph Berger, "U.S. Literature: Canon Under Siege," *The New York Times*, Jan. 6, 1988.

9. *Time for Results: The Governors' 1991 Report on Education* (Washington, D.C.: National Governors' Association, 1986), p. 155.

10. *A Study of Higher Education: Findings Among National Opinion Leaders* (Ithaca: Cornell University Press, 1988).

11. Robert J. Grossman, "The Great Debate over Institutional Accountability," *The College Review Board* 147 (Spring 1988): 5.

12. Allan Bloom, *The Closing of the American Mind: How Higher Education Has Failed Democracy and Impoverished the Souls of Today's Students* (New York: Simon and Schuster, 1987).

13. John Ashcroft, *Time for Results: The Governors' 1991 Report on Education* (Washington, D.C.: National Governors' Association, 1986), p. 20.

14. *Involvement in Learning: Realizing the Potential of American Higher Education* (Washington, D.C.: National Institute of Education, 1984), p. 15.

15. *A New Vitality in General Education* (Washington, D.C.: Association of American Colleges, 1988), p. 52.

16. Peter Ewell, "Assessment: What's It All About?", *Change*, 17, 6 (November/December 1985). See also Pat Hutchings and Elaine Reuben, "Faculty Voices on Assessment" in *Change* 20, 4 (July/August 1988). and Elaine El-Khawas and Jack E. Rossmann, "Thinking About Assessment: Perspectives for Presidents and Chief Academic Officers," Report of the American Council on Education and the American Association for Higher Education, Washington, May 1987.

17. Ewell, "Assessment: What's It All About?", p. 35.

18. *Results in Education: 1988* (Washington, D.C.: National Governors' Association, 1988), p. 39.

19. *A New Vitality in General Education, p. 53.*

20. *Results in Education: 1988*, p. 42.

21. Frank Newman, *Choosing Quality: Reducing Conflict Between the State and the University* (Denver: Education Commission of the States, 1987), p. 7.

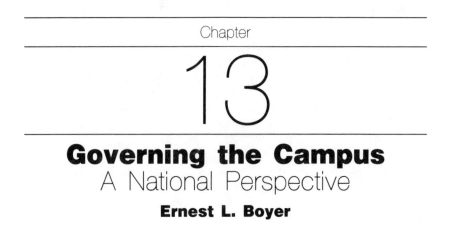

Governing the Campus
A National Perspective
Ernest L. Boyer

Who is to control higher education? This is one of the most important questions confronting the nation's colleges and universities. While many issues relating to governance involve distributions of power and authority on the campus, this chapter focuses on the influences that emanate from outside the institution—especially from federal and state governments and the courts.

In 1981, when the Carnegie Foundation for the Advancement of Teaching began research for our essay on governance, *The Control of the Campus,* a widespread conviction prevailed among educators that the federal government was becoming increasingly intrusive and that conflicts over governance in American higher education stemmed primarily from Washington's meddlesome bureaucracy. At the time I shared these biases, even though I presumably had been part of the problem during my years as commissioner in the U.S. Office of Education, then part of the Department of Health, Education, and Welfare.

But after examining the many charges brought to the foundation's attention during our study, we concluded in our report that the story of the federal relationship to higher education in the United States has been marked more by freedom than intrusion. In the end it was the judgment of the panel that, on the whole, Washington has a record of maintaining a respectful distance from internal campus affairs. Even though the amount of federal support has increased dramatically since World War II, most governmental agencies have refrained from undue intervention. (This point is underscored by any comparison with the far more active involvement of Western Europe's central governments in university matters.)

There are exceptions, to be sure. During my tenure as commissioner of education, we were unable to persuade the Veterans' Administration (VA) to stop imposing detailed regulations on persons receiving benefits under the GI bill. The VA believed that, to be recognized by the VA, academic credit should be given only if students attended class. Further, attendance must be taken. Neither the student nor the campus could be trusted. In a celebrated challenge of this regulation brought by Wayne State University, the courts upheld the right of the VA to define education narrowly and to intervene to an unusual degree. In my judgment, the VA had the wrong notion about the essence of higher education—the assumption was that learning could be measured only by clock hours—and I believe the policies of this agency posed a threat to the integrity of the campus.

Consider a second example. During my tenure in Washington, there was a lively debate about tying eligibility for federal student aid to institutional accreditation. The problem was that self-accreditation, controlled by the colleges themselves, did not ensure that institutions would be well managed. Indeed, the default rate on student loans was very high at many accredited institutions. In response to this problem, it was proposed that the U.S. Office of Education become its own accreditor, deciding through a management audit which institutions were eligible for student aid. To me, this proposal seemed to offer threatening prospects for federal control. It struck me as an ominous move with long-term, negative implications.

A third example of federal intrusion relates to federally funded research and the conflict over legitimate overhead charges by campuses. When the government tried to impose a ceiling on overhead and became involved in the details of how overhead money should be spent, campuses became extremely nervous about the move; charges of federal control were heard. But here the government's view was more defensible, I believe. In my estimation, overhead monies occasionally have been rather carelessly assigned. Universities should exercise discretion in determining overhead costs. At the same time, federal contracting agencies do have the right to inquire into such matters, and institutions of higher education should negotiate in good faith.

A fourth problem I encountered related to the use of federal monies for research involving human subjects: recombinant DNA research is a prime example. If the wrong moves are made, there could be awesome social and health implications. What we confronted, then, was the sensitive issue of developing federal guidelines to control the use of public funds for what could be life-threatening research. Would the federal government be interfering in scholarship? Much credit goes to former Health, Education, and Welfare (HEW) Secretary Joseph Califano for resolving this controversy in a creative way; Califano set up peer review panels drawn from the academy itself. In effect, an intermediate unit—a professional partnership—was established to carry out a legitimate federal responsibility; the chosen strategy protected the campus from direct contact with a governmental agency that threatened to impose its judgment on scholarship within the university.

A fifth example of tension between the university and external institutions relates to the crucial issue of civil rights. Let me cite just two cases to illustrate the point.

In 1980, in *U.S. Department of Labor* v. *Regents of University of California*, the Labor Department was investigating a charge of discrimination on the Berkeley campus. Federal officials asked for permission to remove personnel records from the institution, if needed. This resulted in a confrontation between the Labor Department and the university. The contest was finally resolved when Secretary of Labor Ray Marshall volunteered not to take the records off campus, without conceding the point that the department did, in fact, have the *right* to do so. The result was an uneasy compromise in which the *principle* of control presumably was retained by the federal government while the *practice* was modified to accommodate strongly felt sensitivities on campus.

The University of Georgia was the site of another conflict between the academy and the courts. In a 1981 case, a trial court ordered a professor at the university to reveal his secret vote in a tenure case. Civil rights and equity notwithstanding, the professor maintained that no federal agency or court had the right to require him to reveal how he had voted, and he consequently spent time in a Georgia jail, charged with contempt.

All of these examples, whether in the bureaucracy or the courts, are delicate matters that have prompted conflicts of principles not easily balanced. They illustrate that the university lives in a world of ambiguity, as our society tries through regulations and legal interpretations to reconcile institutional autonomy with individual rights. Indeed, the issue is not, strictly speaking, the *autonomy* of the university; complete autonomy does not exist and, for that matter, it never should. After all, universities have always been answerable to some authority—to the church, the state, or to the various constituencies they serve.

Still, maintaining the integrity of higher learning is absolutely crucial if society is to be well served. The university is a unique institution, a repository of our cultural heritage and a source of the nation's future intellectual and economic growth. Therefore, the academy must be free to direct, without outside interference, those functions that may, from time to time, challenge but ultimately enrich the culture they sustain.

How to protect these prerogatives while still answering to the larger community is the essential challenge. We cannot accept external intervention that compromises the integrity of the institution; neither can a university be insensitive to the legitimate claims of those who must be served. Indeed, the balancing of those competing claims, with occasional tilts in one direction or another, has been achieved, I believe, with great success. Federal agencies in the United States have, in my opinion, been remarkably respectful of the traditions of the academic life.

In recent years, however, the spotlight has shifted from the executive branch of government to the judicial. Increasingly, as I have just stated, the courts have become the point of confrontations between institutional and individual rights. More and more, as individuals seek redress for their grievances, they look outside the campus for relief. And in the days ahead, I suspect that most of the integrity issues facing higher education today will be resolved, not over the bargaining table but in the courts. Because a single legal case can establish a precedent for other institutions, the courts will play an increasingly influential, although indirect, role in shaping the issues of integrity in higher education.

A celebrated southern desegregation case, begun in 1970 as *Adams v. Richardson*, has continued to this day, with successive departmental secretaries serving as defendants. At the beginning, the NAACP Legal Defense Fund filed suit against the Department of Health, Education, and Welfare to force cutoff of federal funds to those states found to be in noncompliance with Title VI of the Civil Rights Act of 1964, which bars discrimination based on race. During my tenure as education commissioner, the court ordered HEW

Secretary Califano to produce new criteria to evaluate state higher education desegregation plans. If Mr. Califano failed to do so, he would be held in contempt of court. Despite the fact that the department was acting under an order of the court, Mr. Califano often was subjected to abuse because, it was said, *he* (the courts were never mentioned) was interfering in an area that was the prerogative of the institution.

Recently, the court ruled in this case, now *Adams* v. *Bennett*, that the plaintiffs no longer have legal standing. The repercussions of this dismissal of the seventeen-year-old landmark civil rights case are still being felt, and the decision is under appeal.

I am suggesting that the courts, rather than the bureaucracy, are having a profound impact on the governance of higher education because individuals need a forum to settle their disputes when organizational systems do not work. The courts have an obligation to help maintain the delicate balance between the needs of institutions (which exist, after all, to serve individuals) and individual rights. One hopes, however, that court decisions will also be made with sensitivity to the integrity of higher learning institutions.

Having been involved in the administration of a large public agency, I also am concerned about the interventionist tendencies of state governments. The state role in campus governance involves the legislature, the executive branch, and those quasi-official organizations called "coordinating bodies." In some states, recent actions by these various players have challenged the integrity of higher learning. Certain state legislatures, for example, have adopted the following position: "Since we have less money, we need more control." Such reasoning contradicts basic principles of good management.

If those in government approach their jobs in the spirit of distrust, the system will not work. To engage in effective governance, state officials must assume that most university officials are honest, not dishonest; that they want to do their jobs well, not shirk responsibility; that they prefer to be accountable, not secretive or evasive. While higher education, like every enterprise, occasionally produces scoundrels and scandal, these institutions are guided overwhelmingly by persons of high integrity and goodwill. Relationships with state governments and legislative bodies should be built not on the exception, but the rule, and if public education is to survive and flourish, state agencies must believe in the capacity of institutions to use resources wisely.

The role of coordinating bodies is less clear. While some form of rational planning is required, higher education in the United States now seems to have second thoughts about the benefits that flow from too rigid "master planning" models. After World War II, it was rational to create coordinating agencies to accommodate explosive growth. But these new structures rarely were given the authority needed to "deliver." Moreover, the goals of "coordinators" often were ambiguous. In some instances, state legislatures wanted such bodies to do the tough jobs they themselves were not willing to accomplish: cut budgets and tackle difficult political problems. This is asking too much of any agency—especially one that does not have authority to act.

On the other hand, the campuses want the coordinating bodies to "make sure we get all the money we need and keep the politicians a safe distance away!" Clearly, not only was the move toward coordination marked by overexpectations, it confronted contradictions, too. It is no discredit, then, to coordinating agencies that they could not meet all of these demands.

My own view is that the coordinating agencies can achieve change only by exercising what might be called "moral authority." To the extent that coordinating council leaders are seen as having independence and wisdom, they will be listened to and supported— not because of their legal authority, but because of their wisdom and perspective.

Thus, we should no longer be naive about the role of coordinating bodies as the power broker that will fit all of the pieces together; few if any bodies have the mandate or the authority for this to be achieved. But neither should we dismiss the coordinating role. We still listen carefully to wise people when policy debates are complex and intense. And I believe this is precisely when the coordinating voice can and should be most influential.

Finally, there is the matter of self-regulation in higher education. The Carnegie essay on governance concluded with the assertion that, in the end, the integrity of the campus will be sustained or eroded, not so much by what others do outside, but by what is done—or not done—within the academy itself. I am suggesting that maintaining internal integrity in higher education rests squarely on the shoulders of the campuses themselves. And yet, on most campuses today we have allowed governance to unravel. In the absence of credible internal structures, campuses extend an invitation to states, the courts and the federal government to intervene.

I do not want the excesses of the 1960s to reappear. Still, in the midst of clashes over Vietnam and a host of other issues, there were during those troubled times campus-wide discussions and, at times, imaginative efforts to reform the governance of universities. Some campuses developed remarkably creative experiments in campus decision-making, and yet today, on many campuses, one cannot find a trace of these ideas.

And as I go from one college to another, I'm impressed that higher education appears not to have new and imaginative ideas about how the institution should be governed. Today, in an era of scarce resources, each special interest group on campus attempts to defend its own turf. What we urgently need are forums in which the transcendent issues can be carefully considered. We need governance arrangements that make it possible for students, faculty, and administrators to reach beyond their separate boxes and create a climate in which the whole is greater than the separate parts.

There are, in fact, several areas of concern in higher education where more campus-wide leadership is urgently required if external intervention is to be avoided. First, consider college sports. In recent days the newspapers have been full of athletic scandals. Restoring a sense of integrity and balance to campus athletics is an area where colleges should seize the moment, assert their independence, and demonstrate their capacity for self-governance. Congressional legislation already has been introduced to force institutions to be more accountable for the academic performance of their athletes. Whether this bill or similar interventions will be enacted will depend on the ability of institutions to develop their own effective models for their sports programs. In this regard it is encouraging to see that a committee of faculty members has been convened by the American Association of University Professors to explore the role of faculty in the governance of athletic programs, and junior colleges have decided to strengthen academic standards for their athletes.

Colleges and universities also need to rethink their involvement in the lives of their students outside the classroom. Incidents involving underage drinking—one resulting in the death of a freshman fraternity pledge at Rutgers University in New Jersey—are bringing local prosecutors and criminal courts onto the campus.

The Rutgers incident prompted state legislators to hold hearings and consider legislation regulating fraternity life and campus drinking policies. Again, administrators should assume a more creative role in matters of campus life and governing student behavior if they are to avoid further state and judicial interventions. I am suggesting that there will always be those who want to wrest control from higher education but, when all is said and done, the strength of the university will be determined by the strength of the internal decision-making structures.

In the search for new governance arrangements, I do not suggest a single model for all campuses. Indeed, the longer I think about the matter, the more I am inclined to believe that different decision-making models are needed for different issues—arrangements that range from the formal, legally sanctioned structures of collective bargaining for certain narrowly defined issues to the informal conversations with colleagues that occur in the faculty lounge. In the past colleges and universities have all too often tended to assume that the governance process must be either all *formal* (and consequently rigid) or predominantly *casual* (and often not accountable). But is it possible to take the wide-ranging agenda of higher learning and impose on it wide-ranging governance arrangements, different decision-making strategies to be tied to different issues?

The State University of New York, pursuant to state law, established collective bargaining about the time I became chancellor. While the university did not endorse the move, I felt obligated to make the system work. In New York State it appeared to be to the advantage of everyone in the public sector to establish salaries and working conditions through the process of collective bargaining with the state government. On the other hand, if the scope of collective bargaining had been extended to a wide variety of other decision-making arrangements that fell within the legitimate purview of the faculty senate, the result in my opinion would have been destructive.

But during that period, the university was able to retain both collective bargaining and a faculty senate, plus, of course, ad hoc committees and informal conversations.

My purpose is not to praise or condemn collective bargaining. Rather, it is to illustrate the fact that in one state where collective bargaining became law, higher education's task was to ask "What is legitimate to debate in a *formal* fashion? What should be decided in town meetings of the faculty senate? What should be left open for individual and committee discretion?" Again, I am convinced that sustaining a range of options is the key to good governance in higher education.

One final point. I believe that issues of governance relate, in the end, not to structures but to people. During the Carnegie Foundation's 1983 study of the high school, I was struck by the fact that teachers were feeling discouraged because they were unable to influence institutional policies. And in the current school reform movement, I worry that statewide commissions and legislatures are telling schools what to do—and they do not listen. Meanwhile, teachers are left with more regulations imposed on them, but less involvement. Stripped of dignity and control, morale declines.

In 1987 the Carnegie Foundation published a companion study called *College: The Undergraduate Experience in America.* We surveyed faculty members from coast to coast and completed on-site visits at thirty public and private campuses. Twenty-six percent of the faculty surveyed reported that their college was very important to them, while almost three times as many—76 percent—said that their academic discipline was "very important." Faculty members also consistently reported that they have less control over their environments than a comparable sample of faculty members had reported ten years earlier.

I am suggesting that an organization is healthy to the degree that people are involved and believe the system is responsive. Apathy is not just accidental. If campus governance is ineffective, if faculty do not serve on committees or if students do not vote in their elections, it suggests that people feel powerless to control their environment. If, however, colleagues in higher education can re-capture the conviction that their involvement makes a difference— if they believe that the institution is, in fact, responsive—governance will, once again, become a vital topic in higher education. And, to the extent that governance reasserts itself as a priority on the agenda, institutional integrity will be preserved, colleges and universities will be healthier places to work, and, above all, the goals of teaching and learning on the campus will be enhanced.

Index